WANTS, WISHES, AND WILLS

FT Press

FINANCIAL TIMES

In an increasingly competitive world, it is quality
of thinking that gives an edge—an idea that opens new
doors, a technique that solves a problem, or an insight
that simply helps make sense of it all.

We work with leading authors in the various arenas
of business and finance to bring cutting-edge thinking
and best-learning practices to a global market.

It is our goal to create world-class print publications
and electronic products that give readers
knowledge and understanding that can then be
applied, whether studying or at work.

To find out more about our business
products, you can visit us at www.ftpress.com.

WANTS,

A Medical and Legal Guide to Protecting Yourself

WISHES,

and Your Family in Sickness and in Health

AND WILLS

Wynne A. Whitman, Esq.
and Shawn D. Glisson, M.D.

FT Press
FINANCIAL TIMES

Vice President, Publisher: Tim Moore
Executive Editor: Jim Boyd
Editorial Assistant: Pamela Boland
Development Editor: Russ Hall
Associate Editor-in-Chief and Director of Marketing: Amy Neidlinger
Publicist: Amy Fandrei
Marketing Coordinator: Megan Colvin
Cover Designer: Alan Clements
Managing Editor: Gina Kanouse
Project Editor: Betsy Harris
Copy Editor: Karen A. Gill
Senior Indexer: Cheryl Lenser
Compositor: Nonie Ratcliff
Proofreader: Language Logistics, LLC
Manufacturing Buyer: Dan Uhrig

© 2007 by Wynne A. Whitman, Esq. and Shawn D. Glisson, M.D.
Published by Pearson Education, Inc.
Publishing as FT Press
Upper Saddle River, New Jersey 07458

FT Press offers excellent discounts on this book when ordered in quantity for bulk purchases or special sales. For more information, please contact U.S. Corporate and Government Sales, 1-800-382-3419, corpsales@pearsontechgroup.com. For sales outside the U.S., please contact International Sales at international@pearsoned.com.

Company and product names mentioned herein are the trademarks or registered trademarks of their respective owners.

Disclaimer Required by IRS Circular 230

Unless otherwise expressly approved in advance by the undersigned, any discussion of federal tax matters herein is not intended and cannot be used 1) to avoid penalties under the Federal tax laws, or 2) to promote, market or recommend to another party any transaction or tax-related matter addressed.

Printed in the United States of America

First Printing May 2007

ISBN 0-13-156898-1

Pearson Education LTD.
Pearson Education Australia PTY, Limited.
Pearson Education Singapore, Pte. Ltd.
Pearson Education North Asia, Ltd.
Pearson Education Canada, Ltd.
Pearson Educatión de Mexico, S.A. de C.V.
Pearson Education—Japan
Pearson Education Malaysia, Pte. Ltd.

Library of Congress Cataloging-in-Publication Data

Whitman, Wynne A.

  Wants, wishes, and wills : a medical and legal guide to protecting yourself and your family in sickness and in health / Wynne A. Whitman, and Shawn D. Glisson.

    p. cm.

  Includes index.

  ISBN 0-13-156898-1 (hardback : alk. paper) 1. Medical care—Miscellanea. 2. Self-care, Health. 3. Medicine, Popular. 4. Medical care—Law and legislation. I. Glisson, Shawn D. II. Title.

  RC81.W3653 2007

  362.1—dc22

                    2006101571

To our loved ones, who fulfill our wants,
wishes, and wills every day.

Contents

Section III: The Wants, Wishes, and Wills of Your Medical-Legal Affairs

Section VI: The Wants, Wishes, and Wills of Your Legacy

Acknowledgments

Like most authors, we're incredibly indebted to many individuals who offered guidance, support, assistance, and wisdom throughout the inception and creation of *Wants, Wishes, and Wills*.

We'll begin with Doris Michaels and Delia Berrigan Fakis for having faith in our project. The wisdom and advice from Jim Boyd, Russ Hall, and Dr. Cynthia J. Smith have been instrumental in taking (okay, we'll admit!) complicated medical and legalese and making it accessible to everyone. We also appreciate the patience and expert editing of Betsy Harris and Karen Gill—thank you!

Then there's the input from friends and family alike, including Jeremy Pearce, Rita Pearce, Reverend Monsignor Daniel S. Hamilton, Mary Joan Sheridan, Chris Luongo, Tracy Benson, Joe Gazdalski, and Ronald J. Greenberg, as well as the many individuals who completed our surveys. We'll never be able to thank you enough!

The support of Renato V. LaRocca, M.D., and Jennie D'Angelo at the Kentuckiana Cancer Institute has been invaluable. We also owe Stephanie Pearl Glisson a big thank you for being tolerant, thoughtful, and just plain terrific! But most of all, special thanks go out to Stacy Whitman, Whit Whitman, and Sally Whitman for their wise words, sage counsel, and expert editing. We wouldn't have finished this book without you. Thank you for everything you do!

About the Authors

Wynne A. Whitman, Esq., is a practicing attorney in Morristown, New Jersey, who specializes in tax, trusts, and estates. She advises individuals and families on ordering their legal affairs to ensure their wants and wishes are carried out and their loved ones cared for. She has worked extensively with families trying to put the pieces together after the death of a loved one who failed to organize his or her affairs, including many 9/11 victims. She's also the coauthor of *Shacking Up—The Smart Girl's Guide to Living in Sin Without Getting Burned* (Broadway Books, 2003), which offers relationship, legal, and financial advice to cohabiting women. Ms. Whitman has made appearances on numerous television and radio programs, including *CBS Marketwatch* and *CNN Financial*.

A leading medical oncologist and hematologist, **Shawn D. Glisson, M.D., F.A.C.P.**, provides the most current options to patients with tragic prognoses. A formerly trained minister for the churches of Christ, he is now based in Louisville, Kentucky at the Kentuckiana Cancer Institute, PLLC. Dr. Glisson is a Lieutenant Colonel in the United States Army Reserve Medical Corps; assistant clinical professor of medicine at the University of Louisville; founder of the American Cancer Biorepository, Inc., a charitable cancer research organization; chairman of the Kentucky Cancer Caucus; a member of the American Society of Clinical Oncology's Health Information Technology and Clinical Practices Committees; and chairman of the Quality Committee at Jewish Hospital and St. Mary's Health Care Center. He currently serves as the Commonwealth of Kentucky's representative to the Department of Health and Human

Services' American Health Information Community's Confidentiality, Privacy, and Security Committee.

In their respective professions, Ms. Whitman and Dr. Glisson address life-and-death issues with their clients and patients every day. In this book, they share their collective first-hand experiences and knowledge to guide individuals in sickness and in health.

Foreword

Many songs have been written about the joys of life and living—and the tragedies of losing someone we love. When you listen to those sad songs, you understand that death is indeed universal; it will happen to all of us. Death is in fact part of life, ordered and inevitable—but we human beings much prefer the joyful sounds of life and put off thinking about its end. Nevertheless, those we love and wish to nurture and protect will have to deal with the fallout should we predecease them. This book is an excellent "first step" on the road to peace of mind for you and your families as you make your lifetime plans.

Wants, Wishes, and Wills is written by two people who have intimate knowledge and experience in counseling and helping those who are left behind or may be dealing with the imminent or sudden death of a loved one. Throughout many years as a medical oncologist, teacher, and advocate for patients and legislation to protect and advance their care, I have seen firsthand the devastation that strikes a family who has just heard the diagnosis of "cancer." Though each decade brings new advances in treatment of cancer and other life-threatening diseases, the journey can be exhausting—physically, emotionally, and financially. Being prepared is the best first step to arming yourself, should you or your family face the decisions that must and will be made. And in today's legal and regulatory maze regarding the rights of individuals, your best defense is a good offense. Get ready. Think about what you want, what you wish for—and help make sure that those things will happen—even when you are no longer here to make sure they do.

As you read the sound advice from Wynne Whitman and Dr. Shawn Glisson, think about your own life circumstances. Think about

your family, friends—and yourself. Remember that thinking about its
end may be the most eloquent way to celebrate your life.

—Dr. Joseph S. Bailes, M. D.
Medical Oncologist
Co-Chair, Government Relations Council
American Society of Clinical Oncology

Introduction

We don't plan to get sick. We certainly don't plan to die. But everyone, healthy or sick, will face illness and the end of life, whether we want to discuss the subject or not.

We experience disease, death, and dying every day. It's often the lead story on the local news. It's the newspaper account of a horrific accident or the killing of a local serviceman overseas. It's the obituary of an entertainment legend. We whisper quietly about our neighbor, friend, or colleague with cancer. We're often consumed by the tragedies of others.

But many of us can't talk about, acknowledge, or plan for our own infirmity and mortality.

We can laugh and make light of the subjects, however. We jokingly say, "Just kill me" when facing a long meeting or an encounter with an obnoxious relative. We order "Death by Chocolate" at our favorite restaurants. We refer to an attractive woman as "drop-dead gorgeous." We read the Darwin Awards—an annual listing of the dumbest ways people have met their deaths. At the water cooler, we chat about who was "whacked" on *The Sopranos*. We pass along the latest joke after a tragedy. We refer to death as "buying the farm," "kicking the bucket," "pushing up daisies," "biting the dust," and "corking off," instead of calling it what it is. Death.

But our own death? Our own loss of health? These topics are often off limits. They're too frightening, too depressing, too real to think about. We simply don't want to go there.

Throughout ancient civilizations, much of life was spent anticipating and preparing for illness and death. Health and restoring health were important cultural activities. Tombs were built for Egyptian rulers decades before their final breaths. Beautiful Greek cities were built in an attempt to restore health and ward off death.

Today, modern civilization may be more advanced, more educated, and more efficient, yet we often lack the foresight of our forefathers. Although we might spend money on business succession planning and life insurance, we still fail to acknowledge that illness is likely and that death is inevitable. We fail to talk about disease. We fail to plan for the end. We fail to share our wants, wishes, and wills with our loved ones.

All of us *want* the best potential health care, *wish* for the best possible medical treatment, but *will* have the best outcomes only if our health care is planned. We *want* to care for our families when we die, we *wish* great things for their future, but we *will* only have these results if we plan. Unless you're in the medical profession, it's difficult to know how to make decisions about health and medical matters. And if you aren't in the legal profession, it's difficult to know what to do today in case you get sick or die tomorrow. As different as medicine and the law may seem, they join forces in times of sickness and health, as well as death.

Planning for illness and death is the last thing most of us want to think about. But plan we must, whether by necessity in the case of a terminal prognosis or upcoming surgery, or by diligent, old-fashioned organization and preparedness. For the super-courteous, questioning a medical decision may seem disrespectful. For the superstitious, writing a will invites death. We have our own theory—failing to plan for illness and death invites tragedy. We may visit our doctors and dentists for annual physicals and examinations, but we rarely review our affairs. (Let's face it, we all know how people feel about spending time with lawyers!)

As a doctor specializing in the treatment of cancer and an attorney with an emphasis in estate planning and administration, we know disease and death are scary, sad, and overwhelming. We understand how your medical care and your legal affairs are intertwined. Every day we work with people who learn that their deaths, or that of a loved one, will be sooner rather than later. We know first-hand the fear and anxiety facing these individuals and families. For this book, we also surveyed and interviewed hundreds of healthy people to learn what's important to them. (We've quoted many, changing their names but not their ages.) Not surprisingly, the sick and the healthy share the same apprehensions. What will happen to my loved ones? How can I care for them? How can I stay in control of my health care and my finances? *Wants, Wishes, and Wills* answers these questions by providing critical medical and legal information, whether or not the end of life is near.

Understanding your health care, ordering your affairs, planning for a long illness, and preparing for your last days can be complicated, emotional, and confusing. Instead of focusing on what you *can't* control, we believe that focusing on what you *can* control will empower each of you to make the best decisions for you and your loved ones. The goal of *Wants, Wishes, and Wills* is to offer you critical personal information that will help you make wise choices and retain control of your situation. We also help you understand new terms and concepts that may be thrown at you by health care providers, attorneys, and financial planners. Although we can't remove your fear of illness and life's end, we hope to remove some of the angst surrounding the subject by arming you with the information needed to overcome the different challenges that lie ahead.

David Kuhl, M.D., writes the following in his book, *What Dying People Want*:

> ...dying, like living, presents opportunity for personal growth and development. Dying involves choice. And for some people, the moment of realizing that death is inevitable, that their time is limited, marks the beginning of a new way of being. People generally die as they have lived. They can choose to embrace a particular event, or exist passively as though the inevitable—in this case death—is avoidable.

We encourage you to embrace the unavoidable, to tackle disease and death head on, and to make the choices that will allow you to retain control of your life, your health, and your death.

Wants, Wishes, and Wills is divided into six sections, each of which addresses a different subject. Those of you facing a health care crisis will likely focus on the sections related to health care, whereas others planning ahead will want to focus on the estate planning and legacy sections. Regardless of your current situation, *Wants, Wishes, and Wills* is a valuable resource for you and your loved ones. Because, as we know, everything can change in a heartbeat.

In each of the six sections of this book, there is a chapter dedicated to your wants (what you don't have), wishes (what you desire), and wills (your choices). We recognize that you have needs that must be met. These are your wants. You also have wishes that you hope will come true. Lastly, there are actions you can take that allow you to express your will.

In Section I, "The Wants, Wishes, and Wills of Your Health and Medical Situation," we address the issues of today's patients and their health and medical situations. Gone are the days, if they ever existed, of a family doctor who knew every detail of your personal and family medical history, as well as your concerns, fears, and anxieties. Instead, each patient today encounters a multitude of health care providers, from the clinician performing a diagnostic test to the nursing staff at the hospital to the countless medical specialists required to analyze and diagnose each symptom and determine the best course of treatment. We help you organize your personal health care system, as well as select medical experts and facilities, pharmacies, and programs. Lastly, we outline the different health care conditions—because the more you know about your health, the more you can do to protect it.

Next, in Section II, "The Wants, Wishes, and Wills of Your Personal Situation," we explain how to take charge of your personal situation. You can make a difference in your health care treatment—and we show you useful steps to do just that. Communicating with your providers is critical—we give you tips to improve how you talk with your caregivers. Health counseling and screening can improve your personal situation. So can the drugs, diets, and devices you use.

As the Terry Schiavo case made clear, the end of life isn't always simple. Because Terry was in a vegetative state and left no written instructions as to her care, her family ended up in a protracted and costly legal battle over whether to remove her feeding tube—a question that the courts ultimately decided. Were Terry's wishes carried out? We'll never know. No one can make a decision for you without knowing what you want. With that said, how do you determine what you want? In Section III, "The Wants, Wishes, and Wills of Your Medical-Legal Affairs," we talk about death, the different wishes of patients and families, and ethical dilemmas regarding the subject. There are also different levels of intervention. The importance of learning the distinction between pain intervention and a ventilator to help you breathe cannot be overstated. For those in serious medical situations, learning the different point-of-death definitions will assist you in determining your end-of-life wants and wishes, as well as providing guidance to the loved ones you've selected to carry out your intentions. We explain Living Wills, Health Care Proxies, and Powers of Attorney and how to select the individuals to carry out your wishes. We also discuss why you should communicate your wishes to your loved ones.

Our communities depend on the goodwill of strangers in the time of crisis. The medical community is no exception. Whether you're undergoing a routine procedure or a biopsy or you're the victim of a tragic accident, a donation of your organs or tissue can bring immeasurable benefits. In Section IV, "The Wants, Wishes, and Wills of Your Selfless Contributions," we explain how this works and how you can be a participant, or, alternatively, explain how you can be sure your desire not to be a donor is followed. We also talk about donating your time and energy to the many organizations needing your help. Lastly, we update you on informed consent, donation ownership, and record keeping.

Whether death is anticipated or unexpected, what happens next for many families is an unknown. Section V, "The Wants, Wishes, and Wills of Your Estate Planning," explains the process of estate administration to help remove the anxiety that many face. With that foundation, we explain estate planning and what you can do to simplify the administration process, reduce taxes, care for loved ones, and share your good fortune with charitable organizations. A comprehensive discussion of different estate planning vehicles (such as wills and trusts) is included.

Finally, we discuss the importance of leaving instructions for your loved ones and creating your legacy in Section VI, "The Wants, Wishes, and Wills of Your Legacy." We encourage each of you to take the time to share with your loved ones your hopes, goals, experiences, and personal history. Having the courage to confront death and share your thoughts and fears isn't easy, but for those facing life's final chapter, it's what they want and need. Leaving letters of guidance regarding children, as well as lessons of love and other valuable information, provides assurances and directions to those left behind. We want to encourage you to do everything possible to ensure that your wants, wishes, and wills are carried out in every situation. Lastly, we explain the legacy of your medical safety, rights, and records.

Wants, Wishes, and Wills is about just that: your wants, wishes, and wills. It is not about what you, your loved ones, your health care providers, or your attorneys think you *should* do. It's quite simply all about *you* and what *you* want. We often have patients and clients stating, "I don't know what I should do." Our response is always the same, "Do what you want, not what you think you should do." The end of life is not the time to be worrying about social conventions, hurt feelings, proper etiquette, or pleasing others. It's the time to decide what you want and to take the necessary actions to be sure that your desires are carried out. We think of *Wants, Wishes, and Wills* as a toolbox. We provide the necessary background information to help you evaluate your situation and then build a plan to accomplish your goals. You'll find checklists, resources, and Web sites, as well as additional suggested reference materials and a glossary at the end of the book.

Both of us help people deal with death and disease every day. We meet with patients and clients who know that death is not only inevitable, but close at hand. We know your questions, your fears, and your concerns. We know that understanding and planning can give you control, and from control comes peace of mind.

That's why we've written this book—to share with you our knowledge and to give you the tools you need to confront disease and dying. We use humor and honesty, tales and tributes, facts and figures, information and ideas. You may find our approach irreverent at times. But sometimes a little levity makes the subject easier. And that's our goal.

Wants, Wishes, and Wills is a valuable resource for personalizing your health and legal information. This book is not, however, a substitute for a health care plan and legal advice tailored to your particular situation and circumstances. It's important to have legal documents prepared by an attorney in the state where you reside. It's also critical to consult with appropriate medical specialists regarding your health care.

Like it or not, we're all going to die. We need to acknowledge it, talk about it, and plan for it. As one client of ours stated, "You cannot die smart unless you live smart." You live smart by planning. You die smart by having planned. Reading *Wants, Wishes, and Wills* is the first step to doing just that.

Section I

The Wants, Wishes, and Wills of Your Health and Medical Situation

You've heard the proverb, "Early to bed and early to rise makes a man healthy, wealthy, and wise." Most agree that we feel better and may be much more productive after a great night's sleep. But what about those late-night talk show hosts? They seem healthy, they're certainly wealthier than most of us, and while we can't measure their wisdom, they've got more wisecracks than all of us combined.

Understanding your health and medical situation is much more complex than eating an apple every day or following your favorite old wives' tales. The days of one-stop health care and relying on someone else to look out for you from birth to death are long gone. Today's health system requires you to be proactive and to take charge of your well-being. You need to create your own personal health care system. You need to find the best medical experts and facilities for you and your health care situation. Whether you're in sickness or in health, you need to understand your conditions and options.

Our goal in Section I is to show you how to do all of this. We provide you with a new, personalized method of understanding your health and your health care. Think of it as a map to navigate today's crazy health care maze. You begin by taking everything you know about your health care, no matter how complicated or technical it seems, and breaking it down into your own personal health care system. Next, we help you select your providers and facilities. Lastly, we help you think like a doctor. We outline the information your physicians need that you can and should provide to improve your health and medical situation.

1 ———————————————

Health and Medical Wants: Your Personal Health Care System

Think for a minute about what makes you different, what sets you apart from the crowd, what makes you unique. Look around your workplace, the doctor's office, or the grocery store. Each person is as individual as you are. That's why one person's health care shouldn't be the same as another's and why it's important to create your own personal health care system.

A Guide to Creating Your Personal Health Care System

Today, we look to a variety of health care providers for our health and medical information. And there are so many of them—there's one doctor for this, one for that, and one for something we've never even heard of. The practice of medicine has become more complicated, with cardiac catheterizations, chemotherapies, and corneal transplants becoming commonplace. There's much more to know and many more health care professionals to consult. We long for a single Norman Rockwell small-town doctor to tell us everything we need to know about our health care. But the classic, small-town Marcus Welby, M.D., general practitioner who took care of patients from birth to death no longer exists.

Where do you begin? The place to start is by learning the best and most efficient method to manage your health care system, including your providers. Next, you need to recognize the strengths and weaknesses of each provider. No provider can know everything, so you need to identify who can do what when. In this chapter, we focus on the many parts of your health care system and how they work together to provide you with the best possible care.

So what can you do to create your personal health care team? Begin by remembering who you see and for what. Quick—list the names and specialties of all your health care providers. If you can, you're lucky, either because you don't have many health issues or get regular evaluations and treatments by a limited few. Next, because your providers aren't always on call, try to name all their partners. It isn't easy, is it? That's why you need to create a record of your health care providers.

With so many providers, trying to remember every one is a challenge. That's why we've broken down your health care system into the following categories. Follow our list to help you recall the caregivers you rely on to take care of you from head to toe. It's the quickest way to create your personal health care system:

Your health systems:
- Health insurance
- Health resources (other than providers)

Your medical histories:
- Past medical history
- Family history
- Social history

Your beauty regimens:
- Salon
- Cosmetologist
- Massage therapist

Your hygiene routines:
- Preventative medicine and wellness
- Health club
- Nutritionist
- Public health clinic
- Psychology and counseling
- Dentist
- Audiologist
- Optometrist and optician
- Podiatrist

Your healers:
- Physician practice
- Hospital and clinic
- Drug and device development
- Tissue bank
- Organ donation organization
- Alternative therapist

Your convalescence programs:
- Rehabilitation medicine (for example, occupational therapy, physical therapy, speech therapy)
- Occupational health clinic
- Home nursing agency
- Substance abuse rehabilitation center

Your drugs and devices:
- Pharmacy
- Pharmaceutical company
- Prosthetic and device distributor
- Prosthetic and device manufacturer

Your comfort measures:

- Nursing services
- Medical appliances
- Nursing home
- Chiropractor
- Acupuncturist
- Reflexologist
- Disability services
- Hospice

This list gives examples but is not comprehensive. If we tried to list every type of provider, this book would be as long as *War and Peace*. However, all of your health care providers can be placed into one of the preceding eight categories. What's important is including *every* caregiver. Not sure if someone qualifies as a provider? Include that person anyway.

Creating your own health care system helps you account for all of your providers and accurately and efficiently share this information with each member of your health care team. Having information categorized is beneficial to your good health and your treatment, especially during health care crises. Your list should include the name of every health care provider, along with his or her group name, addresses, specialties, and phone and fax numbers. This list may become critical if you're incapacitated and unable to provide this information for any reason. Once you've completed your list, give copies to your health care providers for their records and recommendations. Update your list regularly.

My Personal Health Care Team

Make a list of everyone who is part of your health care system. Include the following information for each provider:

- Name
- Group name
- Specialty
- Address
- Telephone number
- Fax number
- Date of last visit
- Reason consulted

You may be thinking, "Why does my surgeon need the contact information for my dentist?" We can give you specific examples of conscientious nail care experts who alerted a client's doctor to a possible life-threatening infection, a local cosmetologist performing a facial who noticed a suspicious mole and reported the information to a client's dermatologist, and a massage therapist who was concerned about a lump on the bottom of a client's foot that turned out to be a tumor. Sure, these examples may be unusual. But they're important examples of the intricacies of today's health care system. Imagine how much more important it is for your internist to know that you're seeing a rheumatologist or cardiologist. We can give you sad examples of open-heart surgery patients who forgot to tell their dentist they'd been hospitalized and ended up with a fatal infection that could have been prevented with a dose of antibiotics before the dental visit. While your provider will likely tell you of a problem first and let you contact your other providers, if there's an emergency, you want them to know who to call. You need and want everyone to work together.

Your Health Care Records

If you're moving out of town or just moving to a new doctor, you can obtain a copy of your health care records by writing to your current physician and requesting a complete copy of your file. Share this info with your new provider, and add it to your health care records if you haven't already.

Contrary to what you may believe, health care providers, including physicians, don't call each other all the time to compare notes about all their mutual patients. Of course, sometimes there aren't enough hours in the day. In some cases, they might find it helpful, but they don't know who to call. And even if you did mention Doctor B's name in passing, you can't guarantee that Doctor A will remember or wrote it down legibly. (Have you seen most doctors' handwriting?) Sharing your personal health care system is critical.

My Own Interoperable Health Network

Until your health care records are electronically secure and easily exchangeable among health care providers (interoperable) in an easy-to-read manner (personalized), it's up to you to let your doctors know who's who in your health care network. Update your provider list whenever you add or switch doctors. Check your list at least annually for address or phone number changes. Also if you have a health condition that involves seeing more than one doctor, be sure to help them work together. For example, if you have an appointment with your internist one day and plan to see your cardiologist the next week, ask Dr. Internist to send a copy of his report to Dr. Cardiologist before your appointment. This allows Dr. Cardiologist to be fully informed before she steps into the exam room, allowing you to maximize your appointment time. Check with the doctor's staff when you arrive for your appointment to be sure that all reports have been received. If the mail is late,

Dr. Internist's office should be able to fax your report. Unfortunately, the lack of stringent security prevents a quick e-mail. Interestingly, some health care systems (the U.S. military and Veteran's Administration hospitals and clinics, for example) discourage faxing of medical records for security reasons; only hand delivery or snail mail is allowed.

If there's one thing we're hoping you take away from this chapter, it's that being a patient doesn't mean just lying back, sticking out your tongue, and saying "Ahhhhhh." Your health care providers and your doctors are intelligent, diligent, and dedicated, but they're not omniscient or omnipresent. You depend on them, but they depend on you as well. Bottom line: You can be a better patient—and get better treatment—if you communicate with your caregivers and constantly update your personal health care system. This will give you more time during appointments to challenge your providers with thoughtful, well-informed questions and concerns. Your health is your most important asset. You need to safeguard it and invest in it. If you don't have the energy to take on this role, shift the responsibility to your health care representative. (See Chapter 9, "Medical-Legal Wills: Directives, Definitions, and Discussions.") Ask questions, be aware, and provide information. We have, in many ways, the best medical system in the world. Take advantage of it.

Health and Medical Wants

- Assemble your health care team.
- Pass your health care system list to all of your providers.
- Be your health care team's most valuable player!

2

Health and Medical Wishes: Providers, Facilities, and Programs

When we think about our health and medical situations, we think about the times when we're healthy and the times when we're ill. If we're healthy, we're concerned with finding providers that will satisfy our curiosity, keep us well, and make us look great. When we're sick, we're concerned with finding experts who will discover what's wrong and then make us better. The different options and choices we can pursue are incredible freedoms. But with freedom comes responsibility, and that can be a daunting task in taking care of our health. Why? Because when we're free to choose, we're free to choose poorly or well.

A Guide to Medical Experts

The information available today is staggering. Even the most skilled and specialized provider can't know it all. Because it isn't possible for any one doctor to know everything, you need providers in the plural, with different training and specialties to suit your particular needs.

I've Just Been Diagnosed. What Do I Do Now?

Whether you've just been told that you have cancer or you've been diagnosed with the brittle-bone disease known as osteoporosis, getting bad news from your doctor is scary. But now isn't the time to shut down. Instead, you'll want to gather information and, if necessary, start treatment as quickly as possible. Start by asking your physician to explain the problem in detail and ask whether there is a course of action to improve the condition or if it will improve on its own. Find out what specialist you should see to establish a workable plan to improve your condition. Request reading material or resources to better understand your disease so that you can ask the right questions of your health care providers. Diseases found early and treated early have the best chance for cure.

Many people choose a medical doctor based on what they read in magazines or see on TV. Local city magazines, for example, often take unscientific surveys to determine the "best" city doctors and publish the results along with the "best" local restaurants, ice cream shops, and yoga studios. These are subjective lists only. They don't reveal the qualifications and possible conflicts of interest of the individuals voting and the criteria they used in making their selections. These are usually nothing more than name recognition lists, often used for self-promotion of a hospital, magazine, or who knows what.

Or maybe we rely on anecdotal stories from others when making health care choices. We ask our family and friends how they like their doctor, pharmacy, rehabilitation center, or dentist. These folks are trying to help, especially in communities with lots of physicians. Whether we get a referral from our insurance company or from a friend or family member, many health care providers are good at what they do. Can every physician be "the best?" Probably not. But the overwhelming majority is probably best for certain people in certain circumstances. It depends on you and your needs.

There are exceptions, however. Sometimes we're not going to the right place because our particular problems aren't that provider's specialty. Ask questions. Make sure this provider has experience treating your specific condition. The first thing you want to know when you see a new physician is something often taken for granted: Will this physician be good for what you need? How do you know? How do you define "good"?

Office Overview

Let's face it—a doctor's office is crazy busy. There are lots of people poking, prodding, and probing. Here's a quick review of who's who:

Physician (MD or DO)—A medical doctor (or doctor of osteopathic medicine) with a medical degree who is licensed by the state where he or she practices. Many physicians today specialize or subspecialize after completing residencies and fellowships and then passing the necessary board exams.

Physician's assistant (PA)—A medical practitioner who works under the direct supervision of a doctor.

Nurse practitioner (NP)—A registered nurse with advanced training in a particular medical specialty.

Registered nurse (RN or BSN)—A nurse who has completed a two- to four-year degree in nursing, respectively.

Licensed practical nurse (LPN)—A nurse who has completed a one- to two-year training program.

So how do you decide who's a good physician? Start by defining the traits you'd like in a doctor. In medical school, residency, and fellowship studies, all physicians are taught that being well trained, having good bedside manner, and keeping long hours are the most important qualities of a good doctor. We call these qualities the three As: ability, affability, and availability. Because it's difficult for us to assess the ability or affability of a doctor we've never met, most of us choose our physicians by availability.

Second Opinions

Whenever you receive a diagnosis that requires a major medical intervention, such as surgery or chemotherapy, or you question a doctor's findings or explanation, you need a second opinion. A **second opinion** is just that—asking another doctor to evaluate your condition, consider your particular situation, and provide his or her recommendation as to the best course of treatment for you. You should ask for a second opinion if you believe a critical diagnosis has not been well explained or if your condition could be handled by more than one type of specialist or subspecialist. For example, certain heart conditions may be treated by a cardiovascular surgeon or a cardiologist, or localized prostate cancer may be managed by either a radiation oncologist with radiation therapy or by a urologist with surgery. Don't be embarrassed—you're not going behind your doctor's back by asking someone else's thoughts. It's prudent and a smart thing to do.

Certainly, the availability of your physicians is important. None of us wants to travel three hours to the nearest city, wait weeks or months for an appointment, or sit in the doctor's waiting room for hours. But availability takes a back seat to ability in certain circumstances. If you need complicated brain surgery to treat a brain aneurysm, you should be asking the newly introduced neurosurgeon, "Do you think you can help me?" not "Do you have an East End office?" When your life is on the line, you want a doctor with top-notch skills and experience who will provide the best possible care. Availability, while still important, should become a secondary consideration.

When you're picking a new health care provider, don't just pick the first name in your health care insurance book. Instead, ask around and get referrals. Also if you're seeing more than one physician for a particular condition, consider whether they know each other and have a good working relationship. Ask Doctor No if he works with Doctor Yes. If you don't get an answer, check with the doctor's staff. In a time of crisis, you need your providers to be able to communicate with each other. And although we'd like to think they could rise above personal differences, would you be able to?

Another important factor is whether your different physicians have admitting or consulting privileges at the same hospital. Unknowingly, patients often rely on two or more groups of physicians at different facilities. If you see one doctor as an outpatient and are then admitted to a hospital that he or she doesn't visit, you'll be stuck with someone new. During initial consultations with new physicians, ask what facilities they use. Check with your current doctors about the hospitals they're affiliated with, and tell them which one you prefer. Too much time and money is wasted when selected providers are affiliated with different medical systems.

What if My Physicians Don't Use the Same Hospitals and Diagnostic Testing Centers?

Although this isn't a disaster, having all of your care providers using the same facilities is certainly a lot more efficient. Why? If you're admitted to a hospital and your physician doesn't have consulting privileges, he or she won't be able to see you, and you'll have to rely on a new doctor. So what can you do? Find out where each of your doctors has privileges, and try to use that hospital—not necessarily the hospital that's closest to your home.

If you're like most of us, the first thing you do when you're referred to a new physician is check your health insurance directory to make sure the referred doctor is part of your insurance plan. Before you scream and yell that he or she isn't there, check the online directory for your insurance company or give them a call. Better yet, call the business office of the physician you want to see and ask. The directories come out annually and aren't always updated regularly.

Let the Patient Beware!

In every town, in every county, and in every state, there are certain health care providers that, frankly, are bad for your health. Contact your state medical board to make sure that a prospective provider has a license in good standing and doesn't have formal disciplinary actions against him or her. You may also be able to search pending and recent litigation to see if he or she is the subject of multiple lawsuits. Don't be afraid to ask around. If he or she gets bad marks for bedside manner (or worse), you may want to move to the next name on your list.

After availability, affability is the next trait that most of us consider when picking a new provider. During your initial visit, you'll get a sense of the doctor's personality. Ask yourself if it will be easy to get along and talk to this person. You should feel comfortable asking questions, and you should feel as though he or she listens and explains things clearly. If a physician makes you feel uneasy, brushes off your concerns, or seems to speak in another language, then he or she probably isn't the one for you.

Two factors impact your doctor's bedside manner: personality and interests. As part of your bedside manner evaluation, think about your own personality type. The Jung-Briggs-Myers typology is a commonly used tool to assess personality. It classifies people using four criteria. The first criterion, extroversion versus introversion, focuses on the source and direction of energy expression. Because the extrovert's source and direction of energy expression is mainly in the external world, he or she is usually very friendly, talkative, and outgoing.

The introvert focuses his or her energy mainly in the internal world and is usually quiet, contemplative, and shy. You can find both extroverted and introverted physicians.

Sensing versus intuition is the second criterion. It focuses on how a person perceives information. If you're a sensing person, you generally believe the information you receive is from the world around you. If you're intuitive, you believe information you receive is from the internal or imaginative world. Most physicians are more sensing than intuitive.

The third criterion is thinking versus feeling, which looks at how new information is processed. A thinking person makes a decision using logic. A feeling person makes a decision based on emotion. Because most physicians fall within the "thinking" category, this can be a common area of conflict when patients are feeling people.

The last personality criterion looks at what a person does with the information he or she has. A judging person organizes the information, formulates plans, and acts on the plans. A perceiving person is more inclined to improvise and seek alternatives. Once again, physicians usually fall into the judging category.

It's the different combinations of these above four criteria that determine personality type. When you're considering the affability of a potential new doctor, you need to think about the type of personalities you like to be around given your own personality.

With that said, personality types shouldn't be the most important thing because most of us can get along with others, even if they're different. Your physicians' special abilities and particular interests, therefore, may be more pertinent than affability when choosing the "best" physician for you.

Physician "Hats"

Physicians can take on many roles throughout their careers. Understanding your doctor's "hats" will help you determine his or her skill level, interests, what he or she does every day, and his or her ability to understand your particular condition.

Experimental physician—A basic research physician most likely associated with a university, pharmaceutical company, or government agency who spends a great deal of time in a research lab.

Clinical research physician—A research physician who conducts clinical trials and is most likely associated with a large practice or hospital, university clinic, institutional review board, or pharmaceutical company.

Numerical physician—A business managing physician for health payers who is most likely associated with an insurance company, medical product development company, government agency, or Wall Street firm analyzing the industry.

Regulatory physician—An academically oriented physician, often associated with medical societies or government agencies, who is involved with organizing research results, reimbursement policies, or clinical research to set best practice guidelines for institutional and practicing physicians. He or she may also provide organized feedback to numerical, clinical research, and institutional physicians.

Institutional physician—A business managing physician who runs an office practice, hospital staff, or other group of practicing physicians.

Practicing physician—A diagnosing or treating physician who sees patients regularly in an outpatient or inpatient setting. This is the type of physician you're most likely to see.

Generally, it's uncommon to meet an experimental physician in the course of any disease management program. If the disease is rare enough, however, or if the research center is large enough, there's a chance you could interact with such a doctor. If you're interested in getting to the root of the disease you're facing, you might seek out an experimental physician, but don't expect to depend on him or her for nonspecialized problems or to manage your case.

A clinical research physician is usually associated with a large hospital or practice, university clinic, pharmaceutical company, or government research agency. He or she would likely work closely with other clinical research physicians or Ph.D. scientists but may still see patients who have conditions that he or she is researching. The advantage to finding a clinical research physician for your disease is that he or she will likely be one of the most knowledgeable physicians for your disease type. With that said, however, if your subset of the disease isn't what he or she is truly interested in, you probably won't receive as much attention. You'll likely still need a practicing physician to manage your care.

A numerical physician addresses medical issues in business management, often in the private or public health insurance or pharmaceutical industry or in a financial research firm. Most numerical physicians no longer see patients and instead crunch numbers for a living.

A pure regulatory physician is another physician you're not likely to see. Generally, regulatory physicians work with medical societies, government agencies, and pharmaceutical companies, for example, to ascertain the current thinking in the area of his or her expertise. If the subject is, let's say, cardiovascular disease, a regulatory physician may know almost everything there is to know about the current treatments of this disease. Whether a regulatory physician can still take care of you depends on whether he or she is still associated with a group of practicing physicians.

An institutional physician is usually the administrative physician for the practice that you go to. It can be the group's senior physician or the physician with the most business savvy. Because it's a time-consuming job, there may be more than one institutional physician. You can expect that this doctor will be the best resource in understanding the local medical community and the personnel within his or her practice. This doctor can make things happen with the clinical staff and office personnel. Many, but not all, institutional physicians see patients as practicing physicians.

The doctor with the most availability is the practicing physician. If you have complex, multiple conditions that are unrelated to one another, you want a practicing physician who can help you with each of these issues. Check to make sure the practicing physician you see has some involvement with his or her state specialty association because you'll benefit from your doctor's interaction with other experts in the community.

Remember, it's possible, and often the case, for your physician to wear more than one hat. Choose the hat or hats that best fit your circumstances. Don't think badly of your physician just because he or she doesn't wear the right hat for you. Just like the fashion world, certain hats go with certain outfits.

The ability of a medical doctor is determined by his or her background. Ask where he or she was trained. What residency was completed? Was time spent doing a fellowship in a particular specialty? Don't be afraid to make inquiries because you need the answers. Although you can trust that your physician will send you to the right specialist for your illness, you should still ask questions to understand his or her perspective. Remind the doctor who's making the referral about the issues that are important to you before asking for a recommendation. Ask if the specialist is available and affable as you define it. Check to see that he or she is a trained specialist for your condition or conditions. Inquire as to board certifications. Find out if the specialist has had any licensing problems with your state medical licensure board.

Medicine is complex. And because no one medical doctor can know everything, there are specialists and subspecialists for different parts of the body, different illnesses and injuries, and different treatment methods. When you receive a diagnosis, ask the diagnosing physician who you should see and why. Ask for an explanation of the recommended specialty (or specialties) and what that specialty does. Check to see if there is a subspecialist who might be better for your condition. If the diagnosing physician can't suggest a particular specialist, inquire as to how you can find the right specialist for you.

White Coat Cast

A white coat used to mean doctor, and that was all you needed to know. Today there are residents, fellows, specialists, subspecialists, and a whole lot of other physicians (although they don't actually wear white coats all the time!). Here's a quick who's who of the "white coats":

Medical doctor—A medical school graduate who may or may not be qualified by a state, hospital, or with a given specialty or subspecialty.

Physician in internship—A medical doctor in the first year of a one-year accredited residency training program such as internal medicine, general surgery, or family practice.

Licensed physician—A medical doctor who has completed one internship year, passed a state medical licensure board, and doesn't have criminal convictions in any state. A licensed physician without further training in residency or before he or she completes residency training may be referred to as a general practitioner.

Resident physician—A licensed physician or a foreign medical graduate (FMG) of a non-U.S. medical school who is in a residency program for a particular medical specialty. FMGs may receive their state medical license to become a licensed physician after completing a three-year residency, which includes a one-year internship, and passing a state medical licensure board examination, provided he or she doesn't have criminal convictions in any state or other country.

Physician specialist—A licensed physician who has completed his or her residency program in a given area such as internal medicine, general surgery, pediatrics, family practice, and obstetrics and gynecology, for example.

Board-eligible physician—A physician specialist who has completed his or her residency and is eligible to sit for the respective specialty board. If the physician specialist does not pass the specialty board within a set time frame after completing the residency, board eligibility will be lost, and the physician will be considered a non-board-eligible physician specialist.

Board-certified specialist—A board-eligible specialist who has passed his or her respective specialty board exam. An example is a board-certified doctor of internal medicine. Board-certified specialists are the most uniformly and academically qualified physician specialists in the nation.

Physician in fellowship—A board-eligible specialist who chooses to apply and is accepted for a particular subset of study within a given specialty. Fellowships can last from one to four years. For example, internal medicine fellowships include, but are not limited to, cardiology, pulmonology, medical oncology, endocrinology, rheumatology, gastroenterology, hematology, and infectious disease.

Physician subspecialist—A physician who has completed his or her fellowship program.

Board-eligible physician subspecialist—A physician subspecialist is at least board-eligible certified in the specialty governing his or her subspecialty, has completed his or her fellowship, and is expected to take the necessary board examination within the required time frame.

Board-certified physician subspecialist—A board-eligible subspecialist who has passed his or her respective specialty and subspecialty board exam. In the United States, board-certified subspecialists are the most uniformly and academically qualified physician subspecialists. A medical oncologist, for example, is a board-certified subspecialist within the internal medicine specialty.

Even the most dedicated doctors need a vacation. When meeting a new physician, ask about his or her associates because they'll be covering for your vacationing or sick doctor. For example, when a mother-to-be is selecting an obstetrician to deliver her baby, she should interview or inquire about all the doctors in the group because she won't be able to control who will be on call when it's her time to give birth.

What's Up, Doc?

Looking for a new physician? Log onto the Web site for your state's medical board to make sure your prospective doc has a current medical license. Then, before scheduling an appointment, ask the following questions:

- Is he or she in my insurance network? Word to the wise— because your insurance guidebook may not be up-to-date, call the physician's office directly and ask.

- Is this practice taking new patients?

- Is he or she board certified in his or her specialty or subspecialty? This means he or she has received the appropriate training and passed the required exams. Refer to the relevant board specialty at www.abms.org. ABMS (the American Board of Medical Specialties) is a not-for-profit organization representing 24 medical specialties that set standards for medical specialists' physician certification.

- Do this physician and his or her group use the same hospital and diagnostic testing facilities as my other doctors?

A Guide to Choosing Medical Facilities

If you live in an urban area, chances are you have access to a wide range of medical facilities. We'll start with the one we all know the best—the hospital. But there isn't just one type of hospital—there are academic teaching hospitals, community teaching hospitals, general community hospitals, and specialty hospitals.

Academic teaching hospitals are usually affiliated with a university program and emphasize research and teaching more than just serving patients. At these institutions, you may see experimental and clinical research physicians, as well as a lot of medical students and physicians who are in training.

Community teaching hospitals, often larger in size, are usually affiliated with a medical school teaching program. Their focus is patient care, followed by research and teaching.

General community hospitals, found in almost every local area, have no (or a limited) role in training physicians. Their sizes run from small to large. Patient care is their primary focus.

Specialty hospitals concentrate on particular conditions, such as pediatrics, mental health, mobility, rehabilitation, or cardiac care.

Government hospitals (such as Veteran's Administration hospitals) can be found at the federal, state, or local level and can be academic, community teaching, or general community, depending on their government charter and opportunities within the community. A government facility may offer you services at greatly reduced rates if you're eligible, although timeliness and staff availability may be impacted.

Ambulatory care facilities are not hospitals, although they can resemble them. These facilities include outpatient surgery centers, emergency care centers, and medical centers. At an ambulatory care facility, you can't be admitted as an in-patient or for more than 23 hours. The advantage to these facilities is that they're easier to use and often have a more focused purpose. The downside is that a full range of medical services isn't available.

Doctor's offices or clinics may offer medical services in addition to office examinations with your doctor. For example, you may receive chemotherapy treatments, stress and radiology tests, dialysis, or other outpatient services at your physician's office. The benefit is efficiency, ease of use, and generally a friendly, less intimidating environment. Like the ambulatory care centers, a full range of medical services won't be available. Physicians' offices are just that—the place you go to meet your doctor. Some offices provide minor medical services, such as biopsies; others refer you to other facilities if additional medical care is required.

Public health clinics are commonly arranged by each state, through the county system, to deliver health care to the under- or uninsured. Often, public health clinics treat communicable diseases, such as HIV and sexually transmitted diseases. In certain regions of the country, all types of health care are provided, including dental services, eye exams, and care for kids and pregnant women.

Immediate care centers are acute care doctors' offices that don't require appointments. The physicians staffing these centers are often nonspecialists or emergency specialists who make themselves available for minor injuries (a cut finger requiring stitches), acute, non-life-threatening illnesses (the flu), or other ailments that require a doctor's attention but don't warrant a trip to the emergency room.

Convalescent and rehabilitation centers are places where patients are taken to recuperate after a serious injury, illness, or surgery. You often hear of stroke or paralysis victims transitioning from a hospital to a rehab center. Patients who've had knee or hip replacements often spend time in a rehab center before heading home.

Nursing homes are long-term care centers for people needing continuous nursing care, whether it's due to old age, illness, dementia, or injury. Sadly, patients in need of nursing home care are not expected to get better.

So how do you determine what type of facility is best for you? First, talk to your doctor. If you need a minor surgical procedure, an ambulatory care center may be best. Perhaps you need a biopsy; if it's highly focused, your doctor may send you to a specialty hospital. There are different facilities for every need, many with overlapping services. Discuss your options with your caregiver every time. Once you determine what type of facility you need, you may have different ones to choose from. Your doctor may have a recommendation, of course. If cost is an issue, you should check with your insurance provider to find out what facilities are covered by your insurance. The Joint Commission on Accreditation of Healthcare Organizations has a Web site (www.jointcommission.org) with information on accredited facilities. HealthGrades (www.healthgrades.com) uses Medicare mortality and complication data to rate hospitals. Medicare (www.medicare.gov) can help you search for hospitals in your geographic area.

Sometimes you may be governed by your geography, but whenever possible, try not to let this limit you. It may be inconvenient to drive hours to get to a better hospital or testing facility. But if that facility will provide optimal care, it may be beneficial in the long run. Sometimes a little inconvenience is worth it. However, we've also heard reports of people traveling overseas for elective surgery at reduced rates. All we'll say is that you often get what you pay for— and sometimes you don't even get that.

A Guide to Pharmacies

Today, there are at least three types of pharmacies (besides the in-patient pharmacies you find in medical facilities). For starters, there are the ones many of us know and love: the locally owned, Mom-and-Pop drugstores. These small businesses, which are quickly disappearing, often have a pharmacist who knows you and all the medications you're taking. Your neighborhood pharmacist has the ability to personalize your service and often provides home delivery. There's a level of comfort that may make it easier for you to ask questions.

In addition to these Mom-and-Pop drugstores, we also have national retail pharmacy chains, such as Walgreens, CVS, and Rite Aid (the top three chains in North America). Others are emerging and growing fast. The national retail pharmacy chain has consolidated much of the drug delivery industry, which has helped to reduce costs. It has also impacted prescriptions written by physicians by making a state medical license for all practical purposes a national license; you can travel to another state and still have your prescription filled. The new trend among national retail pharmacy chains is to offer nurse practitioners on a regular basis to answer questions and provide minor medical care, such as writing a prescription for a stomach virus or an infected cut, along with annual flu shots and blood pressure monitoring. We believe this is a likely future direction of the practice of general medicine. Just don't forget to tell your doctor that you received medical attention on the run.

Medical Service, Magazines, Milk, and More

With the advent of complicated medical specialties, the local general practitioner is hard to find. For this reason, plus the American love of convenience, we're seeing a merger of the general practitioner with the national pharmacy chains. Pull in to fill your prescription. Even better, talk to the nurse practitioner on duty who may write you a prescription for that persistent cough or upset stomach. Your prescription can then be filled on the spot. First, though, do some double-checking: Confirm that a doctor oversees the providers and that your insurance carrier will cover the service costs. If you use one, make sure that you keep records so you can tell your primary physician—he or she will want to add this to your chart. Keep your eye open for medical service at a drug store near you.

Nowadays, you can also get prescriptions filled by mail-order pharmacies. In most cases, you must provide a doctor's prescription via fax or mail or have your doctor call it in. The benefit to you? You can get your Rx without ever having to leave the house or wait in long lines. However, with mail-order pharmacies, you do sacrifice immediate and personalized service. The Federal Drug Administration (FDA) warns people to steer clear of mail-order pharmacies that don't require a valid prescription. Mail-order drug delivery works well for chronic conditions but clearly won't work if you need a certain drug right away. The cost savings is a big plus, but you'll sacrifice personalized service.

When you go to different pharmacies, there's no record of all the drugs, either prescribed or over-the-counter, that you're taking. As we've said before, any drug you take, no matter how insignificant it may seem to you, is still medical care. Until your health care records are completely interoperable, it's up to you to make them interoperable by telling your doctor everything.

A Guide to Medical Palliation Programs and Hospice

You may be thinking, "What's palliation?" **Palliation** creates comfort for the uncomfortable. It's the treatment of your symptoms, such as pain, to alleviate discomfort. Palliative care isn't the treatment of the disease that's causing the problem. *The sole focus of palliative care is to make you comfortable*, often because further medical intervention has been deemed fruitless by you and your physicians. Hospice is the best example of palliative care for the terminally ill and, contrary to popular belief, it isn't just for cancer patients. You often see palliative care and pain management for those suffering from Parkinson's Disease, ALS, MS, AIDS, and cardiac disease, to name a few.

Palliative care is available at many medical facilities and is often closely associated with hospice programs. Hospice isn't a place; it's a treatment program provided at a hospice facility, in your home, or within another medical facility. The goal of hospice is to provide comfort and care to people suffering from a terminal illness or injury. Hospice is able to administer previously prescribed pain medication as well as drugs for symptoms that haven't occurred yet. Pain is treated to provide the patient with some quality of life even though life's end is near. However, pain treatment isn't the only service that hospice provides. It also addresses a patient's social, spiritual, and emotional needs.

It's this multifaceted approach that makes hospice unique. Patients interact with physicians, social workers, nurses, and even members of the clergy. Although the underlying disease isn't treated, other manageable conditions, such as labored breathing, are addressed. Drugs to alleviate pain are provided, but so is physical therapy if it helps the patient. Hospice is about finding ways to make the end of life better for the patient as well as those around him or her. Counseling and support are offered to care-giving family members. Hospice volunteers often fill in for primary caregivers so they can take a much-deserved break. Martha, age 33, cautions, "You need to be prepared for the harsh reality of the message they deliver—that they are there to prepare the patient and family for death."

More than 3,000 hospice programs are available in the United States today, with most insurance plans including hospice as an insured benefit. These programs are both for-profit and not-for-profit. Hospice, as noted earlier, is available for terminally ill patients only, which means an anticipated life expectancy of less than six months. To participate in a hospice program, you must also agree to a Do Not Resuscitate, or DNR, Order (discussed at length in Chapter 8, "Medical-Legal Wishes: Defining Capacity, Consciousness, and Contingencies"). Do you need a prescription to call hospice? Yes. Ask your doctor. There's also a chance that your physician will suggest hospice first.

The benefits of hospice are incredible. Kathy, age 32, "had an amazing experience with hospice" when her father was in the final stages of brain cancer. "At first, I was angry and very resistant to the concept and thought it was simply giving up. But I quickly learned how incredible the people who work in hospice care are—they are truly angels here among us. Helping someone you love go out in a peaceful way is the last thing you can really do for that person."

Everyone we surveyed that had any experience at all with hospice had similar sentiments.

Hospice, though, isn't for everyone. It's not for you if you don't have a terminal illness. Chronic pain can be treated by a pain specialist (usually an anesthesiologist in private practice). If you have a terminal condition without systematic discomfort and you have good social, financial, and family support, you won't necessarily require hospice. Alternatively, if you're still receiving treatment of your disease in an aggressive manner, even if you've been diagnosed as terminal, hospice isn't for you because hospice doesn't treat your underlying disease. If you've made the decision to battle your condition, it doesn't mean you won't receive pain medication. The alleviation of pain is part of all good disease treatment. Don't be afraid to tell your provider that you're in agony. It's the provider's job to help you deal with your pain. It's also not worth it to take the stiff-upper-lip approach to pain. Suffering needlessly saps your energy, exhausts you, and, at the very least, makes you irritable. Fighting illness is hard work; make sure you save your strength for what's important. Don't waste it on enduring pain.

The decision to call hospice is a delicate balancing act. You either want to continue to explore treatments, or you want to receive comfort measures only. You don't want to call hospice too soon, but you also don't want to forget to call them. It's critical to have serious discussions with your doctor about what you want and what you can do. Before you go on hospice, confirm with a medical specialist to be sure you really need it. If he or she tells you there's nothing else you can do for recovery, it may be time to make the call.

Just picking a doctor or medical facility out of the phone book or from your insurance provider book is easy, but it's not the greatest way to find the best provider, facility, and program for you. Decide what you need, and then ask questions and research your options.

Health and Medical Wishes

- Research different medical experts. Find one who's right for your condition, whom you can work with and talk to.
- Consider second opinions!
- Locate facilities that are right for you.
- Make sure your physicians and providers use the same facilities and testing centers.
- Find a pharmacy that meets your needs.

3

Health and Medical Wills:
Your Medical Conditions

Now that you're a few chapters into *Wants, Wishes, and Wills*, we'll take a moment to ask how you are, how you're feeling, if you're well. We're asked this question every day by our colleagues, our family, and by strangers at the local watering hole. Usually, we respond quickly with a "Fine," "OK," or "Not bad." But when we're visiting our doctors, we need more specific responses to these questions.

A Guide to Determining Your Current Health Status

Providers always ask, "How do you describe your general state of health?" An evaluation of your medical status requires you to look at your past, present, and future. Before you do this, you need to understand the different illness categories.

Generally, the American medical system in the past has been centered on the treatment of acute illnesses or conditions. An **acute condition** is just what it sounds like—an illness that comes on quickly, progresses rapidly, and lasts a short time. Acute conditions might include a severe sore throat, a myocardial infarction, or a newly torn Achilles tendon. When we suffer from an acute condition, we're typically treated quickly, thoroughly, and often very well for that particular problem.

Your Medical Conditions

Acute health condition—A disease or condition for which there is a likely chance of full recovery; it's usually an illness or condition that's abrupt, sharp, and of brief duration.

Sub-acute health condition—A condition exists, but all of the symptoms are not yet evident.

Chronic health condition—A disease or condition for which there is likely no cure but that is not expected to cause death for at least six months or more.

Terminal health condition—A disease or condition that is expected to end one's life within six months; also referred to as **end-stage**.

Today, more focus is being placed on chronic conditions. In past years, though, chronic conditions weren't necessarily well managed. They're more difficult because they often require special providers to coordinate multiple therapies over an extended period of time. The U.S. National Center for Health Statistics defines a chronic condition as lasting longer than three months. Unfortunately, some people with chronic conditions think or behave as if they have a series of acute illnesses when, in fact, they suffer from a chronic illness. It's the past misdiagnosis or mismanagement of chronic conditions (often from patients not doing what they're supposed to!) that has led patients to this conclusion. Often the patient, together with a health care system communication breakdown, inadvertently creates this problem. We'll give you an example. Jane Doe has been hospitalized on more than one occasion for confusion or dehydration due to elevated blood sugar levels. The caregivers at the clinics and hospitals she visits, however, acutely treat only the infection that caused the symptoms. The result: Ms. Doe never discovers the real problem. Jane Doe, it turns out, suffers from a chronic condition called diabetes mellitus, not just a recurring bladder infection. She needs to see a physician in an office or clinic to help her understand and manage her diabetes. This would also prevent many ER visits. The point is, a lot of folks think they have acute conditions when, in fact, they suffer from a chronic condition. You must help your providers by being informative, compliant, and consistent with your health care.

Diabetes, as we saw with Jane Doe, is a great example. If her diabetes had been managed, she wouldn't have been hospitalized. Blood sugar can be controlled, and the resulting acute conditions of dehydration and confusion, for example, can be eliminated or reduced. The incidence of decreased kidney function, heart disease, and hardening of the arteries all increase when you have diabetes. What do a sore on the foot, a mini-stroke, and impotence have in common? There's a good chance they're related to diabetes. People with diabetes can avoid other symptoms by understanding and controlling their disease. In other words, you need to learn if you have a chronic condition and, if you do, what you can do to manage it. Although there are lots of people to help you, only you can take responsibility for organizing your disease management.

What can you do? Talk to your doctor. Sir William Osler, a famous medical professor, taught students to find the unifying condition that explains all the symptoms. Why? It's usually all connected—much like your leg bone being connected to your hip bone. This is why you must tell your doctor *everything*. Prioritize. Explain your most pressing problem first, and then follow up with your other concerns. Not sharing every symptom and pertinent details of previous medical care could result in a failure to connect the dots and find the underlying unifying condition. You may be embarrassed that you've experienced forgetfulness, impotence, or incontinence. Don't be. Tell your doctors. Additional problems result when we only treat episodic conditions instead of discovering and treating the underlying chronic condition, especially because the condition can usually be managed and effectively treated once revealed. A diagnosis of Lupus gave Dave, age 33, a new attitude. Once he learned what was making him sick, he accepted his fate and began looking "at things more positively…it was like I could control my destiny."

You may think of health insurance companies as being the enemy, but they really do want you to stay well. (They, of course, save money when you aren't sick.) That's why some offer wellness programs to keep you in tip-top shape. Others have hotlines and help links with nurses who will assist you in understanding and managing your condition. Insurers can be a great resource, but they won't contact you. It's up to you to reach out to them. Call your insurance carrier to find out more, or log onto its Web site. Humana Insurance, for example, offers *My*Humana Condition Centers, which are a terrific resource to help you or a loved one learn more about preventing, treating, or managing a variety of conditions, such as asthma and diabetes. Your carrier probably offers similar resources.

Although we rely on doctors to help us stay healthy, the greatest responsibility is our own. So listen to your doctor and follow his or her advice. If you've been given a prescription for cholesterol-lowering medication, you need to take it! If you suffer from asthma, stay inside on smog alert days. If high blood pressure is your problem, work on limiting your salt intake. Most of all, use common sense and talk to your doctor.

The final type of condition is one that is considered terminal. Although many doctors are loathe to give an exact prognosis for the end of life, a terminal condition is one that is likely to result in death in less than six months. Today, many practitioners refer to a terminal condition as being the end stage of a progressive disease. The diagnosis of a terminal condition can be important in determining your wishes at the end of life as well as any decision you may make regarding the treatment of your condition.

That's why it's important to learn about your different disease types and the categories they fall into. Charting your unique medical situation is the best way to do this. Map out your health conditions from least to most complicated. (You can use the following chart.) Remember, it's possible to have acute conditions that complicate chronic and terminal conditions. Chronic conditions may coexist with terminal conditions.

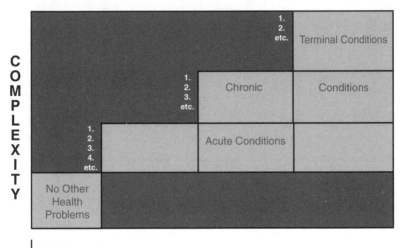

YOUR HEALTH CONDITIONS

If you have no real medical conditions, it's easy. You're in the least complex category in the bottom left of the chart. As your luck fails or you just get older and suffer from more health conditions, your health conditions chart may include a mix of acute and possible chronic or terminal conditions. It's a useful way to analyze what your medical conditions are, how they interact, how aggressive you wish to be with various treatments, and how your other conditions may be affected by your treatments.

The importance of differentiating between disease types has also been recognized for a long time. However, it wasn't until recently that we discovered how to make these differentiations. Think about the second leading cause of death in America: cancer. Should we really say "cause?" Or should it be "causes?" In other words, it's basically useless to ask, "When will they find a cure for cancer?" because cancer isn't one disease—it's thousands, if not more. Other diseases are the same—there are hundreds of infection types, for example.

That's why we can't just think about disease in general categories. Heart disease, the number one cause of death in the United States, isn't necessarily just one problem with your heart—it has to do with your arteries, your blood flow, and other things like your cholesterol. Our point: Until we can break down each disease, we can't fully understand it. And if we can't fully understand it, we often can't fully know what to do to treat it.

We'll give you a brief example. In the treatment of cancer, cell typing became important when it was discovered that a cancer starting in a woman's breast generally behaved differently from a cancer that started in a woman's lung or bone. Even when the breast cancer would go to a lung or bone, it still behaved and looked (under a microscope) like a breast cancer. This is why cancer physicians (oncologists) don't refer to someone with advanced cancer in multiple places as having, for example, breast, lung, and bone cancer, but rather breast cancer that is metastatic (cancer that has spread to other parts of the body) to lung and bone. It may be in different places, but it's still the same kind of cancer.

The stage of a disease is another differentiating factor in treatment. Generally, there are four stages to most cancers, which indicate, depending on cancer cell type, how advanced a cancer is. Stage I is the most limited; stage IV is the most advanced (metastatic). So even after we've found the sub-sub-subtype of a cancer, there are still up to four more divisions of staging to determine. A doctor must

know both the specific sub-sub-subtype of cancer and the appropriate stage to decide the best way to fight the disease.

Understanding your disease type helps you to understand who
you should call and where you should go. It's this fundamental understanding that can make the control and management of your disease
less overwhelming. There's also a degree of comfort in this understanding, especially knowing that, if need be, resources are available
to help you, no matter what your condition. Although there may be
factors out of your control that dictate your disease, your actions can
ensure that the wants, wishes, and wills of your treatment are fulfilled.

Health and Medical Wills

- Understand your medical conditions.
- Make lifestyle changes to improve your health.
- Learn how to manage your medical conditions.

Section II

The Wants, Wishes, and Wills of Your Personal Situation

Because our health is central to our well-being, we want to talk about it. We have questions to ask:

"Is this disease from something I've done?"
"Is this disease like the terrible illness my friend had?"
"Is this a sign of something else?"

We want to know what will work for us especially because what works for us won't necessarily work for you. It's what makes each of us and our personal situations unique.

In Section II, we help you communicate with your doctors. We outline the information you can give to your doctors to help them provide the best possible care. Your physician should talk to you about counseling standards and recommend screening tests. Then there are the drugs you can take. We'll tell you everything you need to know about how drugs are discovered, how they make their way to

41

the pharmacy shelf, and what trials and therapies are available. We'll also talk briefly about the importance of medical diets and medical devices.

Because "the first wealth is health," what do we do when we're in jeopardy of losing it? We become fearful, anxious, and sometimes angry. When we experience serious illness, our very existence is threatened. Our health becomes our top priority. Why? We care about our personal situations. But it's up to each of us to act so that our personal wants, wishes, and wills are fulfilled.

4

Personal Wants: Doctors and Dialogue

No matter what you do for a living, no matter how confident you are, when you're the patient, the sight of a doctor with a stethoscope can make you nervous and often speechless. (And we won't even mention the attractive paper gown you might be wearing!) Learning what you can do to improve communications with your providers is critical to improving your personal health care system.

A Guide to Communicating Better with Your Providers

As you'll probably agree, you may not have enough time with your health care providers to really fill them in on all of your health care concerns and issues in one visit. Even if you have a great relationship with a doctor, you can't guarantee that he or she will be available when you have an unexpected problem. Until your health care records can be electronically stored and transferred among your providers, it's up to you to provide your complete health care information by creating and updating your own records on a regular basis.

Your health care records are made up of your protected health information, or PHI. Recording your PHI doesn't mean carrying around an inefficient clipboard with every paper generated by every provider you see. Instead, it's a road map of your protected health information that should contain answers to the questions outlined in this chapter's headings.

Who Are Your Health Care Providers?

According to the 1999 Patient's Bill of Rights, each patient has a right to have his or her personal physician notified upon admission to a hospital. Although patients have rights, they also have responsibilities. We like to think that our providers are miracle workers, but it's up to us to help them perform these "miracles" by providing our vital information in the form of our personal health care systems. (See Chapter 1, "Health and Medical Wants: Your Personal Health Care System.") Make sure your list includes what you're seeing each doctor for, even if you don't think a certain doctor is relevant to your current problem. Every doctor can tell you that he or she has been called to consult on a patient, only to find that the patient has already been seeing another physician for that particular problem. Talk about a waste of time, money, and opportunity!

Where Were Your Last Tests Done?

Keep a list of the tests you have had, where the tests were taken, and the results (if you know) as part of your PHI Record. Unfortunately, the tendency is to block out negative experiences, which include health care testing. MRIs, CT scans, and biopsies aren't a lot of fun, so it's no wonder we try to forget. But your providers need this information. Without it, your health care delivery can be impaired or time and money wasted with retesting. It's remarkable just how much time and money is wasted because patients can't remember what they had done and where. Be courteous to your physician and kind to yourself. Write down the test information, and bring it with you!

What Medicines Are You Taking?

Telling a physician that you're taking "that little white pill," "a blood pressure pill," "a water pill," or "a sugar pill" really isn't helpful. Sadly, we can recite ballgame statistics and what's on TV tonight but not what we're putting in our bodies each day. If your doctor didn't prescribe it, he or she may not know that you're taking it. And even if your provider prescribed a particular drug, copies of prescriptions get lost.

Here's a real-world example. You go to Doctor A, who puts you on three medications. Doctor B takes you off one and puts you on two more. Doctor C adds another new prescription. Which physician knows what you are taking? The answer is none. Just because you have a prescription doesn't mean you're actually taking the prescribed medicine! More than a few patients overdose on medications by thinking two different bottles are different drugs. Who but a health care professional would really know that Lasix is the same thing as Furosemide? Both refer to the same compound. Take too much, and you may become dehydrated, which could lead to life-threatening kidney failure. Take too little, and your doctor may over-prescribe for you the next time. If only you'd told your doctors and pharmacist everything.

Make sure you mention all natural remedies and alternative medicines you're taking, too. We can't emphasize enough the importance of telling your health care providers about every pill you pop. Remember that aspirin, antacid, and acetaminophen are medications, too. Most people don't take this "full disclosure" seriously. Physicians are constantly frustrated by patients' failures to tell them about all medications, both prescription and over-the-counter. Even the countless patients who wind up hospitalized as a result don't get the message. Do you really have to tell your doctor everything? Only if you want the best medical care possible.

What Exactly Is This Pill?

If you forget to ask your doctor specific information about a prescription, ask your pharmacist for the name of the medication, the dose, and how often and for what length of time you should take it, advises Tracy A. Benson, Pharm D. Then add the information to your medication list. Dr. Benson also says you should "review any medication warning labels the pharmacist has affixed to the container; if any information on the prescription container seems incorrect or is unclear, ask for clarification while you're still at the pharmacy or as soon as you receive your prescription." Use only one pharmacy so that your pharmacist can screen for medicines that could potentially interact with one another and cause adverse effects. The Institute for Safe Medication Practices (www.ismp.org) is a helpful resource as well. Another idea: Bring all of your prescriptions with you to each doctor's appointment. Ask a nurse to help you read the labels and create a list of your prescriptions.

What Are You Allergic To? What Are You Intolerant Of?

Allergies and intolerances are two different things, so choose your words carefully when speaking with your health care providers. Just casually saying, "I'm allergic" to a drug or compound when you're not could deny you important treatments. If you are, in fact, allergic to a particular substance, be sure your health care providers know and it's recorded correctly. Review what's in your chart regarding allergies and intolerances, and make sure the following distinctions are made:

- **Serious medication or substance allergy**—Only those substances or drugs that make our faces, tongues, and throats swell, cause shortness of breath, or result in a severe whole-body rash should be listed under this heading. These conditions are called

anaphylactic reactions and are very dangerous. A person's blood pressure can drop, or his or her airway may become compromised to the point that brain damage or death can occur. We've all heard of people dying from a bee sting or a peanut allergy. It can also happen with some prescribed drugs or substances.

- **Mild allergic reactions**—These allergies, which are characterized by mild rashes or itching, may occur with any substance or medication. These are much more common than serious allergies.

- **Nontolerance**—Often people refer to this as an allergy, but it really isn't. An example is stomach upset from a particular medication. You should be sure to include any intolerances as part of your PHI.

Do I Have to Tell My Doctor Everything?

Yes! Because when it comes to your health, knowledge is critical. Your provider won't judge you if you smoked marijuana every day in high school. And your doctor won't stop seeing you if you report alcohol, tobacco, or drug abuse. Let your physician decide that the bunion removal surgery that you had last year is unimportant. If you were given malaria pills during your African safari last year, your provider needs to know. Unless you're a trained medical professional, the decision as to what's important and what isn't should be made by your doctor, not you.

How Are You Feeling?

Fill your provider in on each ache, pain, bump, lump, and everything else that's troubling you. Start with the reason you're visiting and your chief complaints. Tell your doctor why you're there—he or she won't necessarily know unless you make the purpose of your appointment clear. Not only that, but sometimes physicians forget all the reasons they're seeing you. A friendly reminder when you first see a doctor is never out of line: "As you may recall, doctor, when we met last we discussed A and B and were waiting for the results of tests C and D. E is what's happening to me now. What have you found out?" Next, tell your physician every other symptom. Those details matter.

What's Your Health History?

Your physician needs to hear it all—from your broken leg to your bout with chicken pox to your chronic cough. It's not up to you to decide what's important. If you've seen this doctor before, review your chart to make sure all of your information has been recorded correctly. Information to be included as part of your health history is listed next.

A Guide to Your Protected Health Information

We're telling you all this to improve the way you communicate with your caregivers. We want you to realize that this is the way your physicians are thinking about you. Divide your health care information and your answers to the preceding questions into the areas of past medical history, medications/allergies, family history, and social history.

Past Medical History

- Cardiovascular history—List history of all heart and blood vessel conditions, including hypertension.
- Oncology history—List all cancer diagnoses and treatments.
- Neurologic history—List all brain, spine, and other nervous system conditions.

- Endocrine history—List diabetes, thyroid conditions, and related conditions.

- Obstetric and gynecologic history (if female)—List all pregnancies and deliveries, gynecologic testing history (mammograms and pap smears, for example), and treatments.

- Ophalmologic history—List all eye conditions and treatments.

- ENT history—List all ear, nose, and throat conditions and treatments.

- Pulmonary history—List all lung conditions and treatments.

- GI history—List all esophageal, stomach, liver, and small and large intestine conditions and treatments.

- Hematology history—List all bone marrow, blood, and spleen conditions and treatments.

- Dermatology history—List all skin conditions and treatments.

- Orthopedic and rheumatologic history—List all bone and joint conditions and treatments.

- Renal and urologic history—List all kidney, bladder, and, if male, testicular and prostate, conditions and treatments.

- Psychiatric history—List all psychological conditions and treatments.

- Infectious disease history—List all infections with organism types and treatments.

Medications/Allergies

- Prescribed and over-the-counter drugs
- Severe allergies/mild allergies/intolerances

Family History

- Family illnesses
- Deaths and causes of death of family members

Social History

- Where you work and what you do
- Smoking history
- Recreational drug use history
- Alcohol use
- Eating and sleeping habits
- Exercise habits
- Marital status

Your social history—your occupation, your habits (good and bad), and your support system—is important to your health care provider because it may be an indicator of certain diseases, your risk of certain ailments, and your general well-being.

Take notes, create lists, and write down important things. Now that you know what your health care provider is looking for, come to every appointment prepared. The fewer questions your doctor has to ask you, the more time you have for your questions.

You don't want to miss an opportunity to get answers from your physician, so make a list of questions and bring it to each appointment. If you're worried you'll still forget something, bring a friend or family member with you to prompt you if needed. Take detailed notes in case you have questions later.

Personal Wants

- Improve communications with your providers.
- Prepare your protected health information.

5

Personal Wishes: Screening and Counseling

Some health situations are preordained by our genetic makeup and are out of our control. But many can be managed or improved with careful monitoring and lifestyle changes. (Does an ounce of prevention sound familiar?) In other words, with the help of your providers, you can do a lot to help yourself. In this chapter, we'll tell you who to go to for sound health advice and which screening tests may help you catch problems early.

A Guide to Health Counseling

Whenever you're not feeling well, the temptation may be to research your symptoms on the Internet, ask acquaintances in the health care profession, and tune into every alarming story on the 11 o'clock news, imagining the worse. Or maybe you ignore how you're feeling, rationalizing each ache and pain as the wear and tear of old age, the flu, or an "under the weather" day. Whichever path you follow, the result is the same if you can't obtain sound information and good health counseling.

Part of the problem is the difficulty distinguishing between what information is an exaggeration of the truth and what is closer to the truth. When we're buying a used car, we anticipate hearing some overstatements. When we're looking for health care products and services, we expect to hear a more accurate message. But do we? When we listen to a 30-minute infomercial on television describing medical truths that "the medical establishment doesn't want you to know," do we really think that this is just as reliable as a chapter in an established, peer-reviewed medical textbook? When we see these infomercials, we think of the movie *The Outlaw Josey Wales*. After getting a hard sell from a snake oil salesman who claimed his elixir could do just about everything, Clint Eastwood's character spit tobacco on the salesman's clean white coat and asked, "How's it work on stains?" Hmmm...our question exactly.

Who Do You Go To for Your Health Care Advice?

Your providers. Period. Your best friend, business colleague, or basketball buddy may have a lot to say, but he or she may not have medical expertise or fully understand your situation. So before you try that homeopathic treatment that your sister swears by, talk to your doctor.

That's why there's been an attempt to improve levels of trust with conflict of interest statements. A person in a position of trust has a *conflict of interest* when he or she exercises judgment on behalf of others but also has interests or obligations that might interfere with his or her independent judgment. Conflicts of interest should be avoided or openly acknowledged. Why is independent research important? We need to be sure that all recommendations that result from the research are free from any type of bias, or if there is some bias, we want to be able to take it into consideration. The articles that report research results are technical in nature and aren't usually read by nonexperts; however, the experts you depend on do read and rely on this information. That's why medical societies and their journals are constantly improving and adopting new standards for reporting conflicts of interest.

Articles and books written for the general public, however, aren't under the same scrutiny. They should be. The general public has the right to know any and all possible conflicts of interest that someone writing a health article or book has. We're telling you all this for a simple reason: Beware what you read and beware the source. Although there's a lot of excellent health care information available, there's even more misinformation available. Without these disclosures, we can't be sure of the information contained in many health-related infomercials, books, or articles. In other words, when considering the value of advice, we need to know if that individual has a potential secondary gain as a result of giving his or her advice. We have no problem with someone promoting what he or she works at, produces, or studies. We just want to know more about the person's background so we can make informed decisions.

In addition to knowing about the person who is promoting a treatment, we should know more about the treatment itself. We're all familiar with the disclaimers at the end of pharmaceutical ads on television and radio. Similar disclaimers aren't mandated for so-called "natural" remedies. The largely unregulated vitamin and natural remedies market is allowed to make broad claims, which often are untrue or misleading. There's no requirement to prove these claims. Furthermore, many natural remedies are unsafe in individuals who have certain conditions. For example, women with estrogen receptor positive breast cancer often take natural remedies for their hot flashes. These remedies usually contain natural phyto-estrogens, which actually can promote breast cancer. We bet many of the packages don't make that clear.

Although counseling from outside sources can be helpful, your providers are your best health care resource. That's why the U.S. Department of Health and Human Services (HHS) began working on counseling standards. These studies first became internationally recognized when, in 1984, the U.S. Public Health Service organized the U.S. Preventive Services Task Force (USPSTF) for every significant disease condition. The purpose was to bring health care experts together to determine what counseling healthy people should receive to keep them healthy. Counseling standards are, at the very least, the medical issues that your provider should be discussing with you. They're constantly updated by experts in their given areas of knowledge.

United States Federal Counseling Standards as of 2006

Oncology

Breast Cancer Counseling—Chemoprevention counseling for those at high risk for breast cancer and low risk for adverse effects of chemoprevention, such as a history of endometriosis or a hypercoaguable state, which is a condition where the blood has a tendency to clot too easily.

Ophthalmology

Newborn Vision—All pregnant women should be counseled to deliver their babies at a facility that can prevent Ophthalmia Neonatorum. This is a condition caused by an infection from the vaginal canal at delivery. It can be prevented by a topical ointment applied to the eyes of all newborns to prevent blindness.

Dentistry

Dental Caries—Fluoridated water should be available for all children over 6 months of age. Remember that most bottled water does not contain fluoride.

Nutrition

Obesity—All obese adults should be counseled to lose weight.

Chronic Disease—Those who have chronic diseases should be counseled regarding proper nutrition for their condition.

Cardiology

Coronary Heart Disease—Aspirin therapy should be discussed for all those at increased risk for coronary heart disease to determine if this prophylactic treatment is appropriate.

Hematology

Hypercoaguable State—Individuals who have a history of deep venous thrombosis (DVT), pulmonary embolus (PE), transient ischemic attack (TIA), cerebral vascular accident (CVA), myocardial infarction (MI), or another abnormal clotting event should be counseled regularly.

Orthopedics and Rheumatology

Osteoporosis—Bone density screening should be recommended for females 65 years of age and over (60 and over if there are increased risk factors).

Obstetrics and Gynecology

Breastfeeding—All pregnant women should be counseled to breastfeed their babies for at least three months after delivery.

Neural Tube Defects—All pregnant women should be counseled to take folic acid to help prevent certain types of mental and spinal retardation conditions from occurring.

Social

Tobacco Cessation—All tobacco users are to be provided with tobacco cessation counseling.

Physical Activities—All individuals are encouraged to engage in physical activity several times per week to improve fitness.

That's right, with all that can go wrong with our health, with all the diseases, disorders, and dysfunctions that can occur, currently, these are the only federally mandated general counseling standards that your health care provider is directed to talk to you about according to the USPSTF. This is the health counseling that your providers are as certain about as they can be. You can follow a doctor's counseling recommendations or not. Not doing so, though, could harm your health. If your physician and his or her staff aren't counseling you on these subjects, they're not practicing to the "National Community Standard."

Additional counseling standards exist for three groups: nonpregnant females, pregnant females, and both men and women. As noted earlier, the three counseling categories that exist for nonpregnant females are oncology, hematology, and orthopedics and rheumatology. Many of the counseling standards for these women relate to estrogen. We'll give you an example. Menopausal women lose estrogen production from their ovaries. In a significant number of women who develop breast cancer, estrogen is one hormone that stimulates such cancer's growth. Studies have shown, for example, that the drugs Tamoxifen and Raloxifen inhibit the development of cancer in some women who would have otherwise developed it. Those who are at high risk are advised to take one of these drugs as a preventive measure against breast cancer, unless they're also at risk for a blood clot (which is even more likely in women who smoke). Some postmenopausal women may develop weaker bones because of decreased bone density, perhaps because of the absence of estrogen. That's why a bone density test is needed in those women who are at increased risk for osteoporosis.

The second category of counseling advice to be delivered to you by your doctor is for women expecting a baby. Pregnant women should be counseled to take folic acid, see a qualified provider who can protect her infant from infection, and breastfeed her newborn for at least three months.

The third counseling category is for males and females alike: dentistry, nutrition, cardiology, and social history. These focus on the things that most of our parents told us to do: "Brush your teeth. Eat your vegetables. Don't let your heart get broken. And, get up and do something." Hopefully your parents also told you not to smoke—*anything*.

Of course, health counseling is more complicated than these simple statements. You should also talk to your health care providers for more information.

A Guide to Screening for Health Conditions

In addition to what your physician should talk to you about, there are health screenings that he or she should discuss with you. Screenings aren't for everyone. They're recommended for certain groups for certain conditions based on risk-reward studies (in other words, an analysis of benefits, side effects, costs, and ease of use).

This is also the basis of the health care quality measures being promoted today. This new area of health care research looks at the results of organized clinical trials in an attempt to apply them to specific groups of people. These studies first became internationally recognized in 1984, along with the counseling standards discussed earlier in this chapter, with the creation of USPSTF. A counseling standard is what a doctor should talk to you about. A screening standard is a test that your provider should tell you to have.

Since 1984, there have been few specific recommendations, despite many studies. Screenings, like counseling standards, are a National Community Standard that your provider should follow. The purpose of the standard is to identify which people to screen for particular conditions based on a risk-reward ratio for that person and the society in which he or she lives. Most screening tests that have been evaluated have been rejected as useful for the general U.S. population. For an up-to-date and complete listing of all study findings, along with extensive analyses of all major diseases, log onto the USPSTF Web site at www.ahrq.gov/clinic/uspstfab.htm.

U.S. Federal Screening Standards as of 2006

The following are the screening standards that the U.S. Government recommends. If your health care provider hasn't prescribed these screening tests, *ask*! If your provider won't talk to you about it, it's time to find someone new.

Oncology

Breast Cancer Screenings—The serological test BRCA 1 and 2 should be done if there is a family history of breast or ovarian cancer. Women over age 40 should have mammograms every 12–33 months, with special attention given to women ages 50 to 69.

Cervical Cancer Screening—A Pap smear should be obtained within three years of the onset of sexual activity or at age 21, whichever is first. Pap smears should continue every three years until the age of 65, or if a hysterectomy is performed for benign disease.

Colorectal Cancer Screening—A fecal occult blood test (FOBT), or sigmoidoscopy, dual contrast barium enema, or colonoscopy at age 50 or per the recommendation of a physician based on family history or physical findings.

Pediatrics

Preschool Children (under the age of 5 years)—Children under the age of 5 should be referred to an ophthalmologist if they are found to have signs of the following:

> Amblyopia—The condition of having a "lazy eye" that does not see as well as the other. Over time, if uncorrected, the eye will develop poor vision and usually will result in a "crossed eye."

> Strabismus—The condition of having one eye that cannot focus with the other on an object because of an imbalance of the eye muscles. Over time, it will result in a "crossed eye."

> Defects in Visual Acuity—Poor vision for any other reason.

Psychiatry

Depression—The recommendation is for a physician evaluation that should be completed so that an accurate diagnosis, effective treatment, and good follow-up can be accomplished.

Endocrinology

Hypothyroidism—Congenital hypothyroidism should be screened at birth in every child.

Adult Onset Diabetes Mellitus—Type II Diabetes Mellitus patients should be screened for either high blood pressure (hypertension) or the presence of high blood lipids (hyperlipidemia).

Obesity—All adults should be checked for a body mass index greater than 30 kilograms. For a body mass calculator to test yourself, log on to www.nhlbisupport.com/bmi/.

Cardiology

Abdominal Aortic Aneurysm—All 65–75-year-old men who have ever smoked should undergo testing at least once for an abdominal aneurysm.

Hypertension—All individuals over the age of 18 should be screened for high blood pressure.

Hyperlipidemia—All men over age 35 (over 20 years of age if there is a family history of coronary heart disease) should be screened for hyperlipidemia. All women over age 45 (over 20 years of age if there is a family history of coronary heart disease) should be screened for hyperlipidemia. If an individual's total cholesterol level is elevated or high density lipoprotein (HDL) is decreased, then treatment should begin with oral medication.

Orthopedics and Rheumatology

Osteoporosis—Bone density screening for females 65 and over (60 and over if there are increased risk factors).

Infectious Disease

Sexually Active Females—Women 25 and over or asymptomatic women who are sexually active should be tested for chlamydia. Sexually active women should be tested for gonorrhea.

Pregnant Women—Screenings should include the following:

    Gonorrhea

    Urine for asymptomatic bacteriuria by urine collection at 12–16 weeks gestation

    If 25 years of age or over, asymptomatic chlamydial infection

    Hepatitis B Virus (HBV) at first prenatal visit

    Human Immunodeficiency Virus (HIV)

    Rubella

    Syphilis

For All Individuals—Screenings should include the following:

    HIV, if there is an increased risk for infection

    Syphilis, if there is an increased risk for infection

    Tuberculosis (TB) in any one asymptomatic (showing no signs of the disease), but at high risk

Obstetrics and Gynecology

Rh(D) Antibody—Give Rh(D) Immunoglobulin if Rh(D) Antibody is found in a pregnant woman.

Repeat the Rh(D) Antibody for all unsensitized Rh(D) negative women at 24–48 hours gestation unless the biologic father is Rh(D) negative.

Personal History Screen

Social History Screen (for example, occupation, alcohol use, toxin exposure).

Smoking History—How much and what is smoked.

Physical Activities—The amount of physical exercise each week.

Family History Screen

Breast Cancer History in first- and second-degree relatives.

Ovarian Cancer History in first- and second-degree relatives.

Coronary Heart Disease History in first- and second-degree relatives.

Medicine is made up of many specialties. Along with the general federal screening guidelines, medical specialty societies recommend certain screenings. Unfortunately, not every medical society is in agreement as to who should receive what screenings when. For example, different societies suggest PSA (prostate cancer) screenings for men in different groups, ages, and circumstances. There's a call for the Centers of Medicare and Medicaid Services to consolidate screening advice so that screening reimbursement can be improved, but this hasn't happened yet because risk-reward research hasn't been completed.

The bottom line is that screenings are important and, at the very least, you should get the screenings that apply to you. Penelope, age 59, wishes her diabetic mother would participate in screenings and preventive medicine. Instead of visiting a physician regularly, Penelope's mother waits until it's an emergency and is taken by ambulance to the hospital. This failure to comply harms Penelope's mom, but it also wastes valuable resources, which we all pay for. Ask your doctor, check with your insurance carrier, and consider your family history. Find out what screenings are appropriate for you, and request these tests. If you're over the age of 55, for example, and your doctor still hasn't suggested a mammogram, don't wait until your next appointment. Ask now. Your life may depend on it.

We've loaded you up with a lot of information here. We want you to be aware of the options available. Unfortunately, in today's health care system, you need to ask questions, and lots of them, about counseling, screenings, your options, and everything that concerns you. Use the information contained in this book to assist you in asking the best questions. Take the opportunity to improve your health, especially through health counseling and screenings. Remember, you're the quarterback of your health care team. Start calling the best plays for you!

Personal Wishes

- Understand the different counseling standards. Ask your doctor about them if he or she hasn't asked you.
- Ask your provider about screening tests appropriate for you.

6

Personal Wills: Drugs, Diets, and Devices

When we feel great, we take our health for granted. We don't appreciate our bodies or our well-being until we're injured, ill, or incapacitated. That's when our heads start spinning. We want to know what we can do—right now—to get well soon. That's where this chapter comes in. From experimental treatments to dietary changes, we give you the information you need to improve your prognosis.

Let's start with how your doctor knows what he or she knows. It's not by simply reading books written by older doctors or having some direct communication with the Deity (no, M.D. does *not* stand for Medical Divinity). The word "doctor" originally meant "teacher." Teachers learn by understanding research. Medical information is learned by trial and error. That's why we have research trials. To navigate the health care system today, it helps to understand clinical research trials and alternative methodologies.

A Guide to Drug Discovery, Distribution, and Delivery

In 2002, it took about 14 years of research and $800 million dollars to bring a pharmaceutical drug to market. Unfortunately, this cost has shown no sign of decreasing. Instead, we estimate the cost will exceed $1 billion for each new drug in the not-too-distant future.

Drug discovery is meticulous scientific work peppered with serendipity. Researchers are often looking for one thing but find another. In the development of one cancer drug, researchers discovered that certain formulations had a consistent side effect—cholesterol reduction. The result was the development of an effective cholesterol medication that was originally studied as a cancer-fighting agent. Unanticipated discoveries happen frequently enough to make scientists keep an open mind.

We tell you this because we want you to understand that drug discovery is hard. Failure is more common than success. That's one reason why drugs are so expensive. A drug company has millions and millions of dollars invested in each drug that makes it to your local pharmacy. Not only do they need to recover the funds they've already spent, but they also need this money to discover the next great drug. Many drugs are quantitative leaps forward—something we all benefit from. Other new drugs are just as good as already existing drugs and don't offer new benefits. How society values the drug discovery process and what it can afford isn't the focus of this discussion. Instead, we'll focus more on how and whether you should participate in the drug discovery process.

Research is conducted for a variety of reasons, most commonly to provide more effective treatments for illnesses, such as cancer, heart disease, and diabetes, where more improvements are needed because of the widespread nature of the diseases and their associated high costs. The first thing to acknowledge is something that most of us already know: There are two basic types of health research. There's research in the laboratory and research in the real world. Laboratory research is important, but it's not something that the average Joe or Jane encounters. Research in the real world, which is constantly growing in importance, is something you may come into contact with if you develop certain medical conditions.

Believe it or not, the issue of treatment effectiveness wasn't addressed until 1962. Until then, it was assumed that a product should work. Despite the availability of more complicated treatments, such treatments didn't work in everyone. "Snake oil salesmen" also realized how to make money with fancier packaging. As a result, the U.S. Congress mandated that clinical trials be designed to prove efficacy and the extent of the efficacy. An exception to the requirement of controlled clinical trials for investigational drug regulations was made in the United States in 1987. The goal of the exception was to expand access to experimental drugs for patients with serious diseases and no other treatment alternatives or therapies. Another FDA exception is food products, which we discuss later.

Trial or Study—What's the Difference?

All trials are studies. But not all studies are trials. Trials are invasive, usually involving medications, devices, or other treatments. Studies may involve reviewing previous trials and comparing them to other study results. Trials and studies can be retrospective (done after the fact to generate a hypothesis) or prospective (with the parameters of the trial or study set beforehand).

Over time, research trials were developed to determine which treatments were effective and when. The problem to overcome was the variability in response to a given treatment. The clinical research trial is the oldest form of formalized research. Clinical trials, which randomized people into different groups, were developed to avoid outcome bias. **Randomization** is a process by which subjects in a clinical trial are assigned in no particular order to receive one of the treatments being studied. The development of multiple therapies that showed different responses to different people drove, and continues to drive, the issue of treatment effectiveness.

In all areas of disease research, important and effective discoveries are being made. At the same time, though, there's an increase in the marketing of old-fashioned elixirs (usually made of common food items) as pills, giving unwary consumers the idea that the "pill" version of the snake-oil salesman's product has undergone the same rigors as drug testing. Nothing could be further from the truth. Today's regulations apply only to drugs, not food items. So that supposed wonder drug that's made of garlic, shark cartilage, or coral calcium, for example, isn't regulated, has likely never been tested, and despite its claims, may be totally ineffective.

Listen to the Experts!

Your neighbor may tell you how her third cousin did with Drug "X," or your colleague may share with you her success with some obscure alternative therapy. Although we're sure they're well intentioned, what works for one person doesn't work for all. Disease treatment is individualized, and what cured your neighbor's cousin won't necessarily cure you. Information from unproven sources can make you nuts, increasing your stress and anxiety levels. Stick with your providers, especially the ones trained in your condition. Talk to your doctor, and listen to what he or she has to say—don't listen to someone with "something to sell," whether it's a product or a belief system.

We often hear about terminally ill people participating in clinical trials—often because it's the only option. But it's not just someone who's dying who wants to participate in trials. It's the person who is chronically ill and is looking for a better option, maybe trying a drug in pill form instead of the current IV-only option. Or maybe it's someone who can't get rid of her acne who wants to try a new treatment to make her skin look better. Being a trial participant isn't limited to the desperately ill. Patients participate in trials for a variety of reasons:

- To find a treatment or device that works for them
- To get a free drug or procedure to subsidize health care costs
- To help in the field of medical research
- To meet experts in the field
- To make a few dollars

Regardless of why you participate, your participation is critical to moving research forward.

What If My Health Insurance Won't Cover Some Treatments?

If your health insurance provider won't cover all of the costs associated with experimental or standard treatments (such as travel or time out of work), consider cashing in your life insurance policy. If you have a terminal illness and a doctor's confirmation that you have less than six months to live, you may be eligible for a life insurance policy "Living Needs Benefit." In this situation, the full face value of your life insurance policy would be paid to you while you're living to be used in any way you want. If your prognosis isn't terminal, you may want to inquire into a life settlement of your policy. To be eligible, your life expectancy must be 12 years or less. However, instead of receiving the face value of your policy, you'll receive only 10% to 35% of the policy's face value. Check with your insurance broker and financial planner for more information.

Clinical trials are critical to furthering medical knowledge. But what should you be thinking about when a doctor or research nurse asks you to participate in a trial? Should you follow the standard therapy or allow yourself to be placed on a trial? In the United States, the National Institutes of Health provide a service to help patients find appropriate trials at http://ClinicalTrials.gov. It's a great way to learn what your options are. You may also see newspaper and TV advertisements to participate in trials.

There are six ways a person can be treated for a condition, four of which involve clinical trials. The other two are a standard therapy and an alternative therapy. Choosing the right treatment type depends on your illness, your overall condition, and the effectiveness of existing treatments. If you're faced with a serious condition for which there is presently no known cure or the odds are against its working, you may want to consider other options. We'll discuss each trial and therapy in the chronological order of research and discovery.

You may be wondering, "When should I ask to be placed on a clinical trial?" Before you ask, you need to know if a trial is available, that no standard treatment is available for your condition, and that your physician doesn't disagree with the trial for your circumstances. You also have to be agreeable to the stringent compliance required to be on a clinical trial. In other words, you must be willing to follow strict guidelines, travel if necessary, and participate in extra testing.

Phase I clinical trials are often considered guinea pig trials. This category of clinical research trial is designed to help the researcher, not the patient. The patient/subject has some protections, but if he or she is benefited by this trial, it's just a happy side benefit. After going through tests with single cells or animals, Phase I clinical trials are the earliest trials in the life of a new drug or treatment. It's the first trial in humans and is usually small. The question it's trying to answer is, "What's the correct dose, if any, for humans?" The trial is also researching usage, side effects, and how a patient's body responds to the product being studied.

Online Update

At *thestatus.com*, patients can set up a personalized Web site to keep friends, family, and well-wishers updated on their condition. It's a new way to keep your phone from ringing off the hook!

The first patients (usually 3–7 people) taking part in the study will be given, for example, a small dose of the drug in a predetermined manner. If the response is favorable, the next group of study subjects will receive a slightly higher dose. The process continues with continually larger doses of the drug. Any and all side effects are recorded. The aim of the trial is to look at doses and side effects. Once the side effects are experienced by the majority of the study subjects, the Phase I clinical trial is over. Generally, these trials are conducted at a single medical institution.

People entering Phase I clinical trials often have an incurable disease (such as cancer) or condition for which no other effective treatment is available. They've probably tried most or all of the available treatments. Most won't benefit from the trial. Some may even be harmed. Patients entering Phase I clinical trials must be made aware of the possible side effects. A **side effect** is anything you experience that isn't intended. It's an unplanned consequence of the drug, treatment, or procedure. Some side effects are expected, whereas others are uncommon. A common example might be nausea from chemotherapies. Side effects can range from minor to severe. Even if you're not participating in a clinical trial, you can report your side effects online. Log onto www.fda.gov/medwatch/ to report concerns and side effects. Want to learn more about side effects? Try http://medlineplus.gov. A side effect is different from the outcome of a treatment—which is a treatment's end result and can be either positive or negative. Under certain circumstances, Phase I clinical trials make sense for a patient to enter, often because there's nothing left to try. Discussion with a qualified physician is essential before deciding to enter such a trial.

Phase II clinical trials focus on the patient/subject, but not entirely. Most Phase I trials transition to Phase II clinical trials. After a Phase I clinical trial, the safe dose or method in the "average" human is known. (Just remember—you may not be average.) Phase II clinical trials are done to find out the following:

- If the new treatment has the potential to be proven effective
- The disease types that the treatment effectively fights
- More detail about the side effects and how to manage them
- More detail about the most effective dosage

For a patient with a given disease, a Phase II clinical trial warrants more consideration than a Phase I clinical trial. However, even though these treatments have been tested in a Phase I clinical trial, there are still likely to be side effects, many of which didn't appear during the Phase I trial. It's important to remember that it's a *trial*. Just because it's new and your doctor is offering it to you doesn't mean it will work. Of course, when you're facing a tough disease, the standard treatment may not work either. Your physician and study coordinator want you to know this. They want—and are required to get—your *informed* consent. This is your authorization to participate.

Unlike Phase I clinical trials, Phase II clinical trials are often conducted in more than one treatment facility. Each facility will have its own principle investigator and research nurse. It's wise to meet these individuals before getting involved in the study, although it's not always necessary. Why? You want to feel comfortable with your researchers.

If a Phase II clinical trial helps enough of the patients/subjects to reach a statistically significant level of effectiveness, the treatment regimen may transition to a Phase III clinical trial.

You might be wondering if you have to pay for a clinical trial. It depends. Because Phases I, II, and III clinical trials often study unapproved drugs and devices, you and your insurance company may not be billed for those items. If you're being asked to pay for an unapproved study drug, think twice because the research may not fall within the medical mainstream. Because a Phase IV clinical trial studies a drug or device that already has FDA approval, your insurance company and drug company should pick up the tab.

Phase III clinical trials are used to quantify a treatment's effectiveness when compared to the standard treatment, which by definition is the best currently available treatment. A Phase III clinical trial may be constructed in a variety of ways and may compare

- An additional treatment with the standard treatment
- A completely new treatment with the standard treatment
- A new method of giving a standard treatment

Phase III clinical trials involve more than one treatment facility. Sometimes these trials involve thousands of patients in many different hospitals and clinics, often throughout the world. Phase III clinical trials must be randomized. In other words, the researchers place the subjects being studied into groups at random. One group receives the new treatment and the other the standard treatment. Remember again (and many patients forget), *just because it's the new treatment doesn't mean it's the better treatment*. Remember, it's called a clinical *trial* for a reason.

When you receive the standard treatment, your physician is treating you "according to the literature," in other words, pursuant to a successful Phase III clinical trial or the standard practice that hasn't been challenged by new trials. Once a drug or device is approved for use in the United States, it was found to be better, or at least as good as, a standard treatment and therefore becomes a standard treatment. At that point, a licensed physician may use that drug or device in any fashion he or she thinks is best for a patient. Your physician should be providing the standard treatment option to you, if available.

A patient will know he or she is receiving the standard treatment in the following ways:

- **Package insert**—This is the drug label that the FDA has approved for the purpose that it originally or subsequently reviewed. You may read the package insert by requesting it from your physician or pharmacist. You may also get a bound copy of all drug package inserts in the current *Physician's Desk Reference*. Many drugs are studied further over time and are used for conditions or diseases that the FDA did not originally approve.

- **Insurance reimbursement or payment**—When a drug or device is considered a standard treatment, insurance should cover its cost. If the treatment is new, insurance plans may not yet have caught up with the innovation. If this is the case, your doctor may need to contact your insurance company provider to supply the needed documentation. Usually two articles in peer-reviewed journals are required. Your physician's state specialty society should be able to help your physician make these contacts. Your state's specialty society will have a Carrier Advisory Committee (for drugs) and a Durable Medical Equipment Regional Carriers Committee (for devices) for your physician to contact.

Is a Clinical Trial or the Standard Treatment Right for Me?

As with everything, the answer depends on you and your particular circumstances and conditions. With that said, though, you should consider the following:

- Is there a standard therapy or an available Phase IV clinical trial that your physician thinks is best for you? If yes, that's the way to go.

- If there's no standard treatment or Phase IV Trial, is there a Phase III clinical trial available? If it's available, your doctor agrees it may help you, and you're willing to go through the rigors of the trial, give it some serious consideration. It may help you; it's certain to help others.

- If the standard therapies don't work for you and there aren't any Phase IV or III clinical trials, you may want to consider a Phase II clinical trial. Generally, a Phase II clinical trial gives you the opportunity to try something new, although its effectiveness and potential side effects are undetermined. So why participate? Your other options are limited, and you'll be studied by experts in your disease.

- Phase I clinical trials should be your last choice option. Phase I trials are the "guinea pigs" of medical research. Some individuals have no desire to participate in this type of trial, whereas others want to try for the Hail Mary pass or to simply assist in scientific research. No one should jump into a Phase I clinical trial without first exhausting all other options and having a serious discussion with his or her care provider.

- Lastly, there are alternative therapies. By their nature, they've not been proven to work. This doesn't mean they don't work, but we're not sure they do. As with everything else, if you're trying this, tell your doctor! Remember, he or she needs to know everything. Make sure you receive full disclosure from anyone asking you to participate in an alternative therapy study. There's a higher potential for fraud because these therapies are under-regulated.

Phase IV clinical trials take place after a drug or device has been shown to work and licensing approval has been received. A governing body, such as the FDA or the company that makes the drug or device, continues the study of a standard treatment to determine

- More about the side effects and safety of the standard treatment

- What the long-term risks and benefits are

- How well the standard treatment works when it's used more widely than in a clinical trial setting

Participating in a clinical trial is a big decision. Before you sign up, make sure you ask lots of questions, including the following:

- What is expected of me?
- Will I be required to keep detailed records?
- Will I be required to travel?
- What additional testing will be required, and how invasive are the tests?
- What side effects are you aware of to date?

We caution you to ask questions before accepting free drug samples from your doctor's office. It's not because these drugs aren't right for you; it's because sometimes the old standard treatment is fine and the new drug, without a generic equivalent, won't offer new benefits. Inquire as to why the new, sample drug is right for you. Ask how it's different from drugs already on the market. Many of you may not care; however, if you have to pay part of your prescription drug costs, a new drug versus a generic drug could be a budget breaker.

The terms **alternative** or **complementary** are used to refer to nontraditional methods of diagnosing, preventing, or treating disease. Many patients believe that these therapies relieve symptoms or side effects, ease pain, or enhance their lives. If an alternative therapy is proven in a Phase III clinical trial to be effective, it too becomes a Standard Treatment. By definition, it would no longer be an "alternative therapy." Alternative therapy is often distinguished by its holistic methods, which means that the doctor or practitioner treats the "whole" person and not just the disease or condition. In alternative medicine, many practitioners address patients' emotional and spiritual needs as well. This "high-touch" approach differs from the "high-tech" practice of traditional medicine, which tends to concentrate on the physical side of illness.

When we wander the aisles of our grocery store or local health food store, we see large sections of shelf space filled with bottles that

look like they belong in the drug store. Then we notice the name of
the section: alternative medicine. Alternative (or complementary)
medicine generally includes any healing practices that aren't part of
mainstream medicine. If it hasn't been tested and there's no known
anatomic or physiologic mechanism that can be found, the practice is
considered alternative. It doesn't mean they're wrong; it just means
they're unproven. Despite the lack of evidence, several practices now
being used—for example, massage therapy and chiropractic care—
are considered helpful therapies by some physicians and patients.

What Exactly Is Alternative Care?

The National Center for Complementary and Alternative Medicine at the National Institutes of Health recognizes seven general
areas of alternative care (some of which have been put through rig-
orous scientific testing, but many have not):

- **Alternative medical systems** generally fall outside the con-
  ventional medical system of doctors and hospitals. They
  include

  - **Acupuncture**, the practice of stimulating points on the
    body (usually with a needle) to promote healing.

  - **Traditional Oriental medicine**, which focuses on diagnos-
    ing disturbances of energy in the body.

  - **Homeopathy**, treating health problems with diluted sub-
    stances.

  - **Community-based healers** like midwives, herbalists, and
    practitioners of Native American medicine.

- **Herbal remedies** include a range of plants used for medicine
  or nutrition. They're available in grocery stores and health
  food stores or through herbalists and usually come in the
  form of teas, capsules, and extracts. About one-third of American adults regularly take some sort of herb, anything from a
  cup of chamomile tea to soothe nerves to the popular herb
  Echinacea to fight a cold. The FDA does not regulate these

substances. Because herbal remedies aren't rigorously regulated, there are no extensive tests before they hit the market. When we buy a bottle of our favorite herbal capsules, we don't really know what we're getting because the amount of an herb can vary from pill to pill, with some capsules containing much less of the active herb than stated on the label. Depending on where the herb originated, there may also be other plants mixed in the capsules. Herbal remedies don't have to adhere to a standard of safety and quality like prescription drugs do.

- **Manual healing** treats medical problems by manipulating and realigning body parts. Perhaps the most widely known methods are

  - **Chiropractic care**, which focuses on the nervous system and adjusting the spinal column (the bones that encase the spinal cord).

  - **Massage therapy,** which treats the body by rubbing, kneading, patting, or similar touching, to stimulate circulation, increase suppleness, and relieve tension and muscle soreness.

  - **Osteopathic medicine**, which uses manipulation in addition to traditional medicine and surgical treatment.

  - **Healing touch**, in which practitioners place their hands on or near the patient's body toward which, adherents believe, they direct energy.

- **Vitamin and mineral supplements** are often taken by people with chronic conditions such as kidney disease or other conditions. Some may be harmful for other conditions such as excessive doses of folic acid in lymphoma.

- **Mind-body control** focuses on the mind's role in conditions that affect the body. Hypnosis, a sort of conscious sleep or trance, can help some people deal with addictions, pain, or anxiety, whereas psychotherapy, meditation, and yoga are used for relaxation. Many people also turn to support groups and prayer to cope with an illness or feel more connected to others.

- **Bioelectromagnetics** is based on the idea that electrical currents in all living organisms produce magnetic fields that extend beyond the body and can be used for our benefit, treating wounds and osteoporosis in some cases.

- **Drugs and vaccines** that have not yet been accepted by mainstream medicine are also considered alternative. Eventually, after extensive testing and approval by the FDA, some of these medications or vaccines may become regularly prescribed treatments.

While you may not see alternative therapies in your local doctor's office, there has been an increase in integrated health care centers, offering both traditional and alternative care treatments. Your health insurance isn't likely to cover alternative therapies; however, times are changing, so check with your insurer to see if chiropractic or other therapies might be covered. It certainly doesn't hurt to ask. Just remember, share with your doctor every alternative therapy you use, from a high-dose Vitamin C pill to regular chiropractic visits. Not sharing everything doesn't help you and could hurt you.

A Guide to Beneficial Diets

Diets aren't just for those who've packed on an extra 5, 15, or even 55 pounds. In fact, the first two definitions of diet are (1) food and drink considered in terms of its qualities, composition, and its effects on health, and (2) a particular selection of food, especially as designed or prescribed to improve a person's physical condition or to prevent or treat a disease. It's only later that diet is defined as a method to lose weight.

Your diet is important. For certain diseases, a specific diet is required or recommended. We'll give you a few examples. If you suffer from renal failure and you aren't receiving regular dialysis, you need to watch your potassium intake. A low salt diet is important for those with congestive heart failure. Concentrated sugar is enemy number-one for diabetic patients. In fact, a good diet can help some diabetics control their disease without insulin or other medication. Some types of liver and kidney dysfunction require a diet rich in the right types of protein.

Other diseases are also dramatically impacted by what you do and don't consume. If you have a certain type of the rare disease porphyria, for example, you'll not only be intolerant of alcohol, but you'll also need to eat regularly to avoid even mild hunger. This disease can be controlled by diet; however, when undiagnosed, it can lead to psychosis and depression. It can also be an example of a chronic disease being treated as acute illnesses. Another often-undiagnosed condition is hemochromatosis, which is related to a buildup of iron. Hemochromatosis, which occurs in 1 out of 400 people in the United States, can lead to diabetes and liver failure. Gluten intolerance (an allergy to most wheat products) is also under-diagnosed in the United States, but when identified, it can be controlled by limiting wheat-based products. The symptoms of irritable bowel syndrome, or IBS, can improve by consuming dietary fiber.

The next time you grab a can of diet cola, look at the label on the side of the can. We bet your favorite bubbly beverage contains a warning to phenylketonurics, which are persons intolerant of the amino acid phenylalanine. If you suffer from phenylketonuria, or PKU, you have been told since birth (or you wouldn't still be alive) to have a strict diet avoiding that amino acid. Phenylketonuria is a rare, in-born error of metabolism that can cause a buildup of the amino acid phenylalanine, which can cause mental retardation and other health problems. While this is an extremely rare example, we're trying to prove a point. What you consume matters.

If you don't know where to begin, ask your doctor to recommend a nutritionist to make recommendations. He or she will try to help—but you need to ask. Consult Web sites by the specialty organizations for your disease. Log onto www.nutrition.gov for links to Web sites for specific diseases and conditions. Watch out for people who have something to sell—especially when you see ads for weight loss cures. You can control your diet. You might just need a little help. So ask.

Diet also matters with regard to your weight. Every extra pound can impact your health. Weight maintenance and healthy portions are crucial to good health. Because there are entire books and Web sites dedicated to weight loss, we won't address it here. Just know that losing weight and improving your health go hand in hand.

Dietary counseling is important, whether you suffer from a particular disease or simply want to improve your health. It's an easy lifestyle change that is well within your ability to achieve. If you're a diabetic, skip the candy dish. If you suffer from gluten intolerance, pass on the slice of pizza. If you're overweight, don't eat a pint of ice cream every evening. Despite what some people might tell you, there is no food that will cure your disease, but diets can be used to help control diseases and conditions. Keep eating those apples—they may not keep the doctor away, but they are good for you! A few red grapes now and then won't hurt either.

A Guide to Devices

There are many types of medical devices. They range from the devices implanted in your body, such as a pacemaker, to crutches, shower stools, and wheelchairs.

Before a surgeon implants a foreign object in your body, ask questions. Ask what company your surgeon or hospital uses for these devices and how that device compares to other brands. Usually it's determined by the contracts your providers have with device makers and makes little difference; however, it never hurts to raise the question. It may also be determined by the device your doctor believes is the best and is the most comfortable with or which hospital you use.

Selecting the implanted device will rarely be within your control. However, it's still important to inquire about options and outcomes.

You do have control over the standard assistance devices you may need. There are medical appliance stores for these devices, such as walkers and diabetes testing equipment. However, your insurance carrier's reimbursement for such items may determine the device you select. Check with your carrier before you buy.

As with everything we've discussed in this book, you can control your medical care by asking questions. You have the ability to make your own decisions and to implement your wants, wishes, and wills. We encourage you to do just that.

Personal Wills

- Ask your provider about trials and studies for your disease or condition.
- Understand your alternative therapies and tell your physician about them.
- Learn about special diets and how they can help you.
- Understand your options regarding medical devices.

Section III

The Wants, Wishes, and Wills of Your Medical-Legal Affairs

From Karen Ann Quinlan to Terry Schiavo, we've all seen the headline-grabbing stories about the struggle to decide whether to continue life support. The issue is compelling and controversial. It's also been the impetus for countless individuals to think about the end of their lives, what they want, who they want to make decisions for them, and how to be sure their wishes are carried out.

You'll hear strong statements from relatives who demand, "Don't keep me alive if I'm a vegetable." Friends will say with all seriousness, "Pull the plug." We get it—it's what they want. But as we always tell people, just saying it isn't enough. You need to put it in writing. And when you do put it in writing, you need to provide specifics about your medical care at the end of life. Why? Because nothing, especially in medicine, is ever simple. There are various contingencies, mental and physical capacities, and particular circumstances to consider. You might want to be aggressive at certain times but passive at other times.

You've already seen in Chapter 3, "Health and Medical Wills: Your Medical Conditions," the different ways of thinking about your possible medical conditions, whether your conditions are acute, chronic, terminal, or some combination of all three. Organizing information about your conditions can help you clarify your thoughts regarding the treatments you want or don't want. Do you want to be treated aggressively and maybe even experimentally? Or do you want to stick with the standard treatment? Perhaps you want no treatment at all. These decisions are yours. However, you can't make wise decisions until you have a sound understanding of your medical situation.

There are also issues related to different levels of capacity and particular circumstances you should address. These are independent factors that should be considered along with your medical conditions. Section III provides you with the details you need to decide exactly what it is you want and wish for and the best way to be sure your will is carried out.

7

Medical-Legal Wants:
Understanding Interventions

When we're sick or injured, we turn to our providers for help. When we call 9-1-1 or run to our hospitals, doctors, and clinics in an emergency, we're asking them to intervene in our situation to make us better, repair our injuries and, in extreme circumstances, simply keep us alive. It's an intervention for our care. In this chapter, we focus on interventions that provide nutrition, give us blood and medicines, help us breathe, restart our hearts, or treat pain. Learning your different options can help you or your health care representative make split-second decisions that reflect your wants, wishes, and wills.

In previous chapters, you learned how to think about your own medical situation, its complexity, and how it's all connected. Now it's time to learn what your physicians and providers can do to improve your medical situation and, in many circumstances, preserve your life. The first thing you need to do is banish all television hospital shows from your mind. Saving your life is rarely just two minutes of CPR and a lot of frantic activity in an emergency room. Instead, it's ventilators, medication, devices, and a whole lot of other complicated stuff.

All this complicated stuff translates into choices. You can choose what you want when. Of course, that's not to say that there aren't limitations (your particular condition might prohibit certain interventions) and an element of luck (you may be taken to a hospital or clinic that can only offer certain interventions). So how do you make your decisions? The best place to start is with a fundamental understanding of your options.

Interventions can be broken down into five categories:

- Airway interventions
- Breathing interventions
- Circulatory interventions
- Discomfort interventions
- Enteric interventions

For each of these interventions, there can be pharmaceutical and mechanical interventions. Pharmaceuticals are used to treat disease or palliate symptoms. Before you take drugs or consent to IVs, ask what you're being given and why. Inquire as to the side effects, if any. You have a right to know, and you *should* know. You also have the right to refuse pharmaceutical intervention or stop its use at any time. Your desires regarding taking medicine to treat your underlying disease at the end of life should be stated in your Living Will and communicated to your providers and representatives. We talk more about this in Chapter 9, "Medical-Legal Wills: Directives, Definitions, and Discussions."

When you're treated with any type of machine, device, or procedure requiring an instrument, it's a mechanical intervention. The most fundamental examples are the use of a ventilator to help you breathe and the use of CPR (cardiopulmonary resuscitation) to restart your heart, including the use of electric shocks (using a defib-rillator) to start your heart. There are also hundreds of other exam-ples, including dialysis, invasive surgical procedures, and oxygen therapy, to name a few.

It's also important to know the implications of the different mechanical interventions. For example, many individuals say that in no way do they want to be placed on a ventilator to breathe. But what if the ventilator is simply a temporary treatment and you'll be taken off of it within a set time frame? Would that change your decision? Maybe. What if feeding and fluids were needed after an accident and not from a terminal condition? It's another distinction that needs to be addressed.

A Guide to Airway Interventions

We've all had the awful feeling of being unable to get air—sometimes when we swallow a drink and it goes down the wrong way. Or maybe you've had that awful experience of having something stuck in your throat, causing you to choke and gasp for your next breath. Chest congestion that comes with a bronchial infection or other causes can make you feel the same way. If you suffer from asthma, you know this feeling all too well. Patients with restricted airways have the same experience.

The purpose of airway interventions is to remove the airway blockage, using drugs or devices. Pharmaceutical products that might be used include **antihistamines** (which reduce swelling by stopping allergic reactions), **decongestants** (which stop the production of mucus), **bronchodilators** (which make the airway expand), or **glucocorticoid steroids** (which stop allergic reactions). Mechanical devices that are used to open a patient's airway include **intubation** (placing a tube in the mouth or nose to keep the airway open),

otolaryngoscopy (evaluating the nose and throat to find out what's blocking the airway), or **tracheotomy** (cutting a hole in the front of the neck to insert a tube directly into the airway).

A Guide to Breathing Interventions

If you're having trouble breathing, you have several options. The option that's right for you will depend on why you can't breathe, your overall medical situation, and your wants, wishes, and wills. Some patients agree to the use of a ventilator but refuse a tracheotomy, which would likely be necessary if the ventilator is needed for an extended period of time (around 14 days). Still others say to keep them on the ventilator for as long as necessary, even if further treatment is futile. The choice is yours. The key is having all the information you need to make the best, informed decision for you and sharing your wants.

Breathing Basics

Receiving adequate oxygen is critical. There are several different methods to help you get the air you need:

- **Nasal cannula**—The small tube that is inserted in your nostrils. This delivers the smallest amount of oxygen.
- **Oxygen tent**—A structure that encloses a patient in bed and provides an oxygen-rich environment.
- **Face mask**—A device that delivers pure oxygen into your nose and mouth.
- **Ventilator**—The mechanical device that assists a patient to breathe by mechanically forcing oxygen into the lungs; also called **artificial respiration**.

A Guide to Circulatory Interventions

Even the most unscientific of us know that it's our blood running around inside us that keeps us alive. Those guys and gals in the white coats refer to this as **circulation**. Circulation can be impaired by injury or illness. Maybe it's a clot, a clogged artery, or a vein damaged in a car accident. Regardless of the cause, circulatory interventions improve how blood and all the other important fluids in our system move from head to toe.

Intravenous fluids can be used to improve our hydration. If we need blood, we can receive transfusions of packed red blood cells, platelets, or plasma and serum protein products. Drugs, such as **antihypertensives** (which lower blood pressure), **antihypotensives** (which increase blood pressure), **antibiotics** (which fight infections), **antiarrhythmics** (which stabilize heart rate and rhythm), and **anticoagulation agents** (which can thin the blood) can also help.

Then there are the mechanical interventions. The one you're most familiar with is probably **CPR** (cardiopulmonary resuscitation). CPR includes everything from basic life support (manual CPR and mouth-to-mouth resuscitation) to **ACLS** (advanced cardiac life support). The interventions also include **pacemakers** (which keep the heart beating regularly), **defibrillation** (shocking the heart to resume a regular heart rate and rhythm), **pericardiocentesis** (draining fluid from the heart sack to allow the heart to beat), **pericardial window** (creating a site to allow the heart sack draining to take place), **hemodialysis** (removing waste products from your blood when your kidneys aren't working), **paracentesis** (draining the abdomen to relieve pressure), and **compression garments** (machine-operated pressure devices that help to increase blood pressure and avoid clots).

For an elderly individual with advanced osteoporosis, CPR may be specifically refused because pressure applied to the chest could result in breaking already-brittle bones. Obviously, mechanical intervention is considerably more invasive than the administration of a drug or medicine through an IV bag. That's why many individuals want to avoid any type of mechanical intervention but agree to drugs and other noninvasive therapies that may prolong their lives.

A Guide to Discomfort Interventions

One of the overwhelming concerns people have is pain. Can they handle pain? How can pain be alleviated? How might treating pain interfere with treating their disease? This focus on pain isn't a surprise; no one wants to be in pain. Just the thought of it, we're sure, has chills running up and down your spine. Unfortunately, pain often accompanies disease and disability. This doesn't mean, though, that you need to take the pain lying down.

The best way to talk about pain relief is by looking at the different types of pain intervention:

- **Surgical interventions**—For example, having a mass causing pain removed, a broken bone repaired, or drugs introduced surgically to reduce nerve pain.

- **Radiation**—Commonly used to alleviate pain in cancer patients even though the radiation, in this circumstance, likely won't cure the cancer.

- **Pharmaceutical intervention**—Using drugs, often derived from the opium family, to alleviate pain. Pain medication can include **sedatives** (which make you sleep), **relaxants** (which make you feel more relaxed), **narcotics** (a very strong painkiller, such as morphine), and **nonnarcotic pain medication,** such as acetaminophen (for example, Tylenol), aspirin, or ibuprofen.

In addition to the type of intervention used, each patient needs to decide how aggressively to treat the pain based on his or her particular circumstances. Generally, if you're of sound mind with no previous illness or you're suffering from an acute illness, you want to receive enough pain medication to alleviate the pain but no more. The same is true for chronically ill individuals. For terminally ill individuals, it's a personal decision. The terminally ill patient needs to decide what's most important to him or her. The issue becomes one of quantity of remaining days versus the quality of those days. Your desire regarding pain medication should be discussed with your doctor and shared with your **health care representative** (the person you ask to make your health care decisions if you can't). We'll talk more about your health care representative in Chapter 9.

Pain Facts

The National Cancer Institute (www.cancer.gov) provides the following facts on cancer pain:

- Cancer pain can almost always be relieved.
- Controlling cancer pain is part of overall cancer treatment.
- Preventing pain from starting or getting worse is the best way to control it.
- Patients have a right to ask for pain relief.
- Patients who take cancer pain medicines rarely become addicted to them.
- Patients don't get "high" or lose control when taking cancer pain medication prescribed by a physician.
- Pain medicine side effects can be managed or prevented.
- Patients do not become immune to pain medication.

Although all pain is different, the same holds true for most non-cancer pain.

The treatment of pain is also known as **palliative care**. According to the National Hospice and Palliative Care Organization, "The goals of palliative care are to improve the quality of a seriously ill person's life and to support that person and their[sic] family during and after treatment." And for the past 30 years, palliation programs have been doing just that. Hospice programs have traditionally been the source of palliative care. Today, though, you can find palliative care at nursing facilities, hospitals, and through some home health care providers.

Contrary to popular belief, hospice isn't a place—it's a methodology. As discussed earlier, it's an approach to caring for terminally ill patients or those facing the end of life as a result of injury by providing compassionate, dignified care to patients. The care that hospice provides isn't limited to medical care and pain management; it also offers spiritual and emotional support to both patients and patients' loved ones. Every individual we surveyed who had experience with hospice had nothing but wonderful things to say about it. (See Chapter 2, "Health and Medical Wishes: Providers, Facilities, and Programs," for more details about the many benefits that hospice can provide.)

A Guide to Enteric Interventions

Enteric interventions help patients receive hydration and nutrition. The *American Stedman's Medical Dictionary* defines **nutrition** as "the process by which a living organism assimilates food and uses it for growth, liberation of energy, and replacement of tissues; its successive stages include digestion, absorption, assimilation, and excretion." In layman's terms, you need nutrition to live. But many who are ill "forget" to eat because they're not hungry. Food must be encouraged. Hydration is even more important because it's difficult to live more than three days without water. (You can live much longer without food.)

The healthy receive nutrition and hydration whenever they chow down and drink up. The sick, however, may need assistance getting life's necessary nutrients and fluids. The unconscious, it goes without saying, need tubes to receive food and hydration. There are also terminally ill patients or gravely injured people who, although conscious, have lost the ability to swallow. How these nutrients and fluids are delivered is referred to as **nutritional intervention**, which is divided into several categories.

The first type of nutritional intervention requires an IV, which provides fluids directly into a vein. When nutrition is required, a simple IV is not sufficient. This intervention is referred to as **TPN**, or **Total Parenteral Nutrition**. In this case, a **PICC line** (a peripherally inserted central catheter placed into a large arm vein), a **central line** (a line placed in one of the large veins in the neck or chest), or a **port** (an implanted device that prevents multiple needle sticks) will be needed to provide the necessary fluids and nutrients. With prolonged TPN, there is a great risk of infection because of the high sugar and lipid content of the IV contents, which is a favorable condition for infections. For this reason, if nutritional intervention may be required for a long time, TPN may not be recommended.

The alternative to TPN is **Total Enteral Nutrition** (TEN). TEN means accessing the GI (gastrointestinal) tract directly using a **PEG** (percutaneous endoscopic gastrostomy) tube. Food and nutrition go right into the intestines, and that makes the process much faster. In addition, the risk of infection is reduced, which makes using TEN the preferred nutritional intervention for long periods, if a person cannot otherwise eat or drink.

Until recently, most patients wanted hydration and nutritional intervention when they were sick or hurt. Today most still do, although many terminally people are specifically stating that they don't want either food or water unless it's for a very short time and death isn't imminent. Part of the reason is a desire of many people not to linger when death is close. Whether you want hydration and nutritional intervention is a personal and sometimes religious decision dependent on your circumstances at the time. The answer will not be the same for everyone. It's also a very important determination. Many states require that your Living Will (discussed in Chapter 9) include specific language regarding your preferences for nutrition and hydration. Talk to your doctor, your spiritual advisor, and your family. Ask questions before you make your decision. Then put it in writing.

Understanding the different interventions helps us make decisions. The decisions to be made are up to us as individuals, but keep in mind that they're also evolving. What you want as a 50-year-old may not be what you want as a 70-year-old. What you want as a healthy person may be different from what people who are suffering or have suffered from a serious illness may want. In making decisions regarding your health care, pick and choose what's right for you.

Physicians and families are constantly concerned over what a patient wants if the patient can't communicate. Loved ones lament over the countless options. The key is to make choices and communicate them to your loved ones and providers both orally and in writing. Analyze the different situations you may face, and make the right determination for you. Be clear. And remember, as long as you're able to make decisions and communicate those decisions, the decisions are yours to make.

In addition to completing your Living Will, we suggest using the following chart to record your wants regarding medical interventions. You should complete at least three of these forms—one for each of the conditions listed at the top of the chart (terminal, chronic, acute). Your answers to how much intervention you want may be different depending on whether a full recovery is expected or not. Think about the treatments you want in each category and then note them on the treatment table on the following page.

			Terminal Conditions
		Chronic Conditions	
	Acute Conditions		
Airway			
Intervention Types		Pharmaceutical	Mechanical
Breathing			
Intervention Types		Pharmaceutical	Mechanical
Circulatory			
Intervention Types	Hydration / Blood Products	Pharmaceutical	Mechanical
Discomfort			
Intervention Types		Pharmaceutical	Mechanical
Enteric			
Intervention Types	Hydration	Pharmaceutical	Mechanical

LIVING WILL INTERVENTION DECISIONS: TREATMENT TABLE

Medical-Legal Wants

- Learn about the different interventions.
- Discuss what interventions are best for you.
- Discuss your intervention wants with your health care representative and health care providers.
- Complete your intervention chart.

8

Medical-Legal Wishes: Defining Capacity, Consciousness, and Contingencies

When we told people we were writing a book that included end-of-life issues, we, not surprisingly, received similar responses: "Isn't that morbid?" "Why would anyone want to read about that?" or "Could you pick a happier topic?" Our answer is always the same—of course, disease and death aren't a barrel of laughs, but the ability to have some say in the matter of preserving your health and maintaining control at your passing is so critical that we couldn't imagine *not* writing this book.

You shouldn't take decisions about the end of life lightly. End-of-life decisions require you to evaluate the many different circumstances you may be in at that time. The reasons to communicate your decisions orally and in writing are twofold. If you express your wishes with specificity, it will be difficult for others to question your wants. Second, if you're incapacitated, you're providing more information to your decision maker to give him or her comfort in what could be the incredibly difficult decision to follow your wishes.

To help you in your analysis, we've broken down the subject into different areas. The first is determining your competence or capacity to make your own decisions. The second is defining some of the medical terms you should know. Lastly, we help you understand the different medical end-of-life points.

A Guide to Evaluating Medical Capacity and Comas

We'll start this discussion with what is probably an obvious point. As long as you're able to make decisions regarding your medical care, these are your decisions to make and your decisions alone. Even if you have a Health Care Proxy appointing someone to act as your health care representative, while you have the competence and capacity to make decisions, you're the boss of your health care.

What exactly is competence and capacity? If you're unconscious, you have neither competence nor capacity. You can be unconscious as a result of anesthesia, injury, or illness. Your unconscious state can be temporary or long-term. Regardless, when you're unconscious, you need someone to make your health care decisions for you. When you're conscious, you can be conscious with competence and capacity or conscious without competence and capacity. Let's take a look at what this means.

Capacity and Competence

Capacity is legal competence or fitness of an individual's mental or physical ability.

Competence is having requisite or adequate ability or being legally qualified or adequate. In legal circles, an individual is considered competent if he or she is mentally able to understand and execute a legal document.

Capacity and competence can refer to legal qualifications (such as being over the age of 18 and able to legally contract, for example) as well as mental capabilities. Any decisions that a person under age 18 makes must be approved by a parent or legal guardian. We'll focus only on mental capabilities.

We'll use the term capacity to include every situation in which you're able to understand your condition and the choices you're being asked to make and to make those decisions. If you're conscious without capacity, you've lost, whether permanently or temporarily, the ability to comprehend and analyze your circumstances, evaluate your options, and make your own decisions. A determination of capacity is different for each individual. A person may have moments of capacity and moments of confusion. We've learned from years of collective experience that we can determine capacity within a few minutes of spending time with a patient or client and that this capacity can also change from moment to moment. What's critical is the capacity to make a decision when the decision making is required.

The reason for a lack of capacity is equally important in determining an individual's decision-making ability. Why might you lose your capacity? There are many reasons. You could be in a state of delirium. **Delirium** is a short duration episode of "acute mental disturbance characterized by confused thinking and disrupted attention."

Alcoholics may experience a special kind of delirium. **Delirium tremens** is a state of violent delirium induced by excessive and prolonged alcohol use. It's often called the **DTs**. An individual suffering from **psychosis** is experiencing a basic derangement of the mind, including hallucinations, delusions, disorganized speech and behavior, and defective or lost contact with reality. Like delirium, periods of psychosis can be short term or long term. During episodes of delirium and psychosis, an individual is conscious without capacity.

A Little Levity

As one of our favorite professors taught us, sometimes you need a little humor to get you through the tough subjects. So here goes. What's the difference between a neurotic, a psychotic, and a psychiatrist? A neurotic builds imaginary castles in the sky, a psychotic lives in those imaginary castles, and the psychiatrist collects the rent.

As our population has aged, we've seen a marked increase in individuals suffering from dementia. **Dementia** is defined as deteriorated cognitive function, often with emotional indifference. Dementia can be progressive, as with Alzheimer's disease, for example. Nonprogressive dementia, which can be caused, for example, by mini-strokes, a vitamin B-12 deficiency, severe head trauma, or prolonged drug abuse, is also common. The degree of dementia, like all forms of capacity, can wax and wane in an individual. Progressive dementia can also transition into a state of minimal consciousness (defined later). The current state and cause of dementia will impact a patient's capacity and, as a result, the ability to make his or her own health care assessments and choices.

There are many individuals who are emotionally, mentally, learning, or developmentally disabled who may or may not have the capacity to make their own health care decisions. A high-functioning disabled individual performs at a level close to that of a nondisabled person, meaning that although disabled, this person has the capacity to make his or her own decisions. Again, the capacity of a disabled person is a determination to be made by those close to that person, including his or her caregivers.

We've all had the unpleasant experience of being around folks who've had one cocktail too many or are in the midst of a drug high. During states of drunkenness or drug use, a person may be conscious without capacity. There are others who react unfavorably to prescribed drugs, which cause them to lose their capacity. And there are certain pharmaceutical interventions, such as sedatives or pain medication, that inhibit someone's ability, at least temporarily, to make sound decisions. For others, extreme pain or illness affects decision-making capabilities.

The loss of capacity, as noted earlier, can be momentary, long-term, or permanent. It can be the result of an underlying illness or injury or a temporary state caused by any one of a number of different factors. As you focus on your health care wishes and desires, understanding the different circumstances when you may need assistance from your health care representative and what you expect him or her to do in those situations is crucial. Your decisions regarding end-of-life care should also consider your future capacity. For some, if you're permanently incapacitated by dementia or injury, for example, you may want no medical care or intervention regardless of the condition requiring the medical care. It's one more thing to think about and communicate.

The medical terms **coma** and **persistent vegetative state** are used frequently in discussions regarding Living Wills and end-of-life decisions. But what exactly are they? And are they the same thing?

A state of being minimally conscious falls within the category, as we've defined it, of medical comas, and it may follow a persistent vegetative state or advanced dementia. If you're minimally conscious, you'll exhibit behaviors that are deliberate and cognitively meditated. You'll have some awareness of yourself or your environment. In other words, your actions aren't just reflexive or unconscious movements. Perhaps you'll be able to follow simple commands, make an intelligible statement, or respond to a yes or no question. To date, there have been no long-term studies regarding recovery from a state of minimal consciousness.

When an individual is in a coma, he or she is in a deep state of unconsciousness. If you're unconscious, you have no awareness of your circumstances, you're unable to experience sensations, and you're not cognitive. You're alive, but you're unable to respond to your environment. A coma can be the result of injury or illness. In some circumstances, a coma may even be temporarily induced by physicians to treat a patient. Some individuals make a full recovery from a coma, whereas others require physical, intellectual, and psychological rehabilitation. In any case, a coma is unlikely to last for more than 2 to 4 weeks.

A persistent vegetative state may follow a coma or occur instead of a coma. If you're in a persistent vegetative state, you've lost higher brain function and the ability to think. You're no longer aware of your surroundings, but, unlike a coma, you still have normal sleep patterns. Like a coma, your lower-brain functions, such as circulation and breathing, continue. You might open your eyes if stimulated, and there may be some spontaneous movements, including some emotions such as crying or laughing. However, like a coma, you'll be unable to speak or follow commands. Many people refer to a persistent vegetative state or a coma as being brain-dead, but this is a matter of interpretation. Remember, the brain is still functioning, just at a very low level. There's a minimal possibility of regaining some awareness after being in a persistent vegetative state. Some may remain in this state for years.

Can you recover from a coma or a persistent vegetative state? The answer depends on the facts and circumstances of your situation. Factors that may influence your recovery are the cause of the coma or persistent vegetative state, the severity of that state, and the amount and location of the neurological damage. Once the immediate medical emergency causing the condition has been addressed, the biggest risk factors become infection, pneumonia, and bedsores, as well as bone and muscle loss. Hydration and nutritional intervention are required to sustain individuals in comas and persistent vegetative states.

Coma Conditions

- **Minimally conscious**—Altered consciousness with erratic, inconsistent responsiveness
- **Persistent vegetative state**—Unconscious with eyes open and little response to the external environment
- **Coma**—Unconscious with no response to the external environment

A Guide to Choosing Medical End-of-Life Points

Just telling your loved ones that you want "no extraordinary" measures to keep you alive or that you want the "plug pulled" isn't exactly guidance. You need to provide specifics. You do this by first considering your various health conditions. (You may have an acute, chronic, or terminal illness.) Next, consider what interventions you want given your circumstances. Lastly, think about the medical end-of-life points, as well as your philosophical, spiritual, and religious beliefs to determine exactly what you want in every circumstance, and tell your health care providers and health care representative.

Within each of the three categories of capacity (conscious with capacity, conscious without capacity, and unconscious), there are different conditions, care, capabilities, and choices to consider. We'll evaluate each one here and will begin with the conditions of each. It you're unconscious, you've lost your ability to want because you're no longer aware of your environment. You're no longer able to formulate new wishes and wills either. In other words, your wishes and wills remain suspended in time—they'll remain as they were the last time you communicated them to your health care providers and representatives.

If you're conscious without capacity, your wishes and wills are also suspended in time. When your capacity is diminished and you're no longer able to make decisions, you're also unable to formulate new wishes and wills. Your last communications as to your health care wishes and wills (prior to incapacity) serve as your direction to your providers and representatives. However, because you're conscious, you can still have wants.

When you're conscious with capacity, you continue to have wants, wishes, and wills and the ability to change your wishes and wills at any moment. We further divide those who are conscious with capacity into two distinct groups: those who have the will to live and those who don't. This distinction is important and explains why some individuals make certain decisions regarding their lives and health care that are drastically different from others.

We'll take a moment now to address individuals who have a loss of will to live even though there is no concurrent death likely. For some, it's simply an overwhelming feeling that life just isn't worth living. We see this often when one spouse dies and the other dies shortly thereafter. We also see it with the very old who simply feel that they've lived life and are ready to move on to whatever may come next. Within this loss of will to live are extremes. One extreme is the individual who chooses to end his or her life by suicide. For others, it's an unconscious act. They let nature take its course or, for many, there is a failure to thrive, which leads to death.

We must contrast these individuals with those who are terminally ill and have a loss of will to live. Some terminally ill individuals refuse additional treatment. This is a personal decision. Others may seek a means to end their suffering, whether at their own hand (suicide) or by a request made to another (euthanasia). If you're considering the last two options, get professional help. Mental conditions that lead to suicide can often be treated. Euthanasia is illegal in every state but Oregon.

No matter what our level of consciousness and capacity, we can be disease free or suffering from an acute, chronic, or terminal condition, or some combination thereof. There are five interventions for care, discussed in the previous chapter, that are based on complications related to restricted airways, breathing, circulation, discomfort, and nutrition and hydration. Deciding whether interventions are right for you is not a simple yes or no question. There may be certain circumstances when it's what you want and certain circumstances when it's not.

Before we move on, we'll give you a quick brain lesson. That place where all your smarts are located is divided into three parts. One part is the brain stem. The **brain stem** governs your basic bodily functions and reacts to the environment. Without your brain stem, you can't live without mechanical help. In other words, you'll need help breathing. This part of the brain also controls your swallowing mechanism. If you can't swallow, you'll need hydration and nutritional intervention.

Then there's the part of the brain that has do with the physical coordination of your movements—your **cerebellum**, or the back part of your brain. You could live without most of the cerebellum, although your coordination would be compromised. We won't focus on damage to the cerebellum for our purposes.

The rest of the brain is your **cerebrum**. This is the most complicated part of your brain. It controls your personality, language skills, vision, memory, actual physical movements, and more. How much and what part of the cerebrum is damaged will dictate the extent of the brain injury. When the cerebrum is damaged, it's all about location, location, location. The challenge is determining the exact location of the injury. Unfortunately, it's not that easy.

We'll begin with the loss of brain stem function. In this situation, you may continue to have capacity to refuse or accept treatment; however, the failure of your brain stem to function means that your body can no longer operate itself without the assistance of machines. For example, you need a ventilator to help you breathe. We often see the loss of brain stem function with high-level cervical spine injuries. Christopher Reeve's brain stem ceased to function after his horseback riding accident, but as we know through his hard work, he retained his capacity for years after his tragic accident.

It's important to address this situation with your health care representative. Think about whether you would want to receive life support in the event your brain stem function was lost. These decisions must be made quickly—often following the accident or medical incident causing the injury. At this moment in time, you probably wouldn't have capacity, due to a loss of consciousness, to decide what it is you want in this given circumstance. That's why you need to rely on your health care representative to make the decisions you would have made, provided you've given him or her your thoughts on this contingency and those that follow. It's also helpful to understand these different scenarios in case you're called upon to make decisions for someone else.

Next we'll address the loss of cortical brain function. This issue became important when our definition of death changed in the 1960s. The change occurred when it became possible to remove a heart from a "brain dead" individual and transplant it into an individual who wasn't "brain dead," but "heart dead." Prior to 1966, death was generally thought to occur shortly after a person's heart or lungs stopped functioning. "Brain death" without heart or lung death is a concept widely accepted in the western world today, but not by all. For those who accept the concept of brain death as a legitimate point of death, we have to ask, "How much of the brain has to be dead for death to have occurred?"

Your **cortical brain** is your higher brain function. There are varying degrees of cortical brain function. In certain circumstances, despite the loss of cortical brain function, you can still have capacity. Therefore, it becomes important not just to measure the loss of cortical brain function but also the level of capacity in making decisions. More often than not, however, you'll have lost capacity, perhaps permanently. If this is the case, do you want assistance being kept alive?

With some brain injuries, there is the loss of both brain stem function and cortical brain function. In this situation, not only has your body lost the ability to act without mechanical intervention, but your cerebrum has also been damaged. As with all brain injuries, there are different degrees and different combinations of the two. Various specialized tests may assist in assessing the extent of injury. However, because many decisions regarding care must be made instantaneously, this testing may not be an option. It also helps to show why simple statements like "pull the plug" really aren't helpful.

Another example of brain injury is the loss of whole brain function, including **neurohormonal function**. We include this discussion for reasons of completeness. Some consider brain death to be the point when hormonal secretions within the brain neurons can no longer be measured. It's when there's simply nothing going on upstairs. There's a single cell test to determine whether someone has brain activity. Others rely on electrocardiograms to analyze brain activity by measuring groups of cells. Clearly, this is extremely complicated. Neurologists and neurological scientists are required to make these determinations and, hopefully, to explain them to a patient's health care representative.

Before the 1960s, the traditional American view of the point of death was the loss of cardiopulmonary function. This was because when either your heart or lungs stopped working, the other would stop shortly thereafter, and the rest of you would die within minutes. However, with modern technology, the ability to keep the heart beating can last from 5 minutes to 5 years and longer. Our ability to save lives for those near death has expanded our options. For example, what happens when the heart remains beating but there is whole or partial brain death? What do you want to have happen? More than half of states (whether by law or court decision) determine the point of death to be when the brain stops functioning and when this condition can't be reversed. But they don't mention how much of the brain has to stop functioning. Brain damage can occur after mini-strokes and after massive head injury. The remaining states still adhere to the traditional view of death, as being when all vital functions have stopped. The question: Where do you draw the line?

Prior to the advent of modern medicine, death was considered the cessation of complete cellular function. Death occurred when rigor mortis occurred and every cell was dead. It remains the point of death in some cultures today, including many Asian, African, and Middle Eastern cultures and parts of the world with traditional medical beliefs. In addition, many of these cultures consider death to have occurred after the point when the family recognizes the physical death, which could be days later.

The Different Points of Death

We include all of the following examples of the different points of death because every person may have a different view of what death means. The government has one version, physicians another, and different cultures and religions may have their own definitions. Our goal is to make you aware of each to allow you to make your own decision regarding what point of death contingencies in which circumstances may warrant the refusal or termination of medical attention for you and you alone:

- **Loss of complete cellular function**—Every cell in the body is dead, usually evidenced by the onset of rigor mortis.

- **Loss of cardiopulmonary function**—The heart stops beating, and the lungs stop oxygenating blood.

- **Loss of whole brain function, including neurohormonal function**—The loss of all brain activity.

- **Loss of both brain stem function and cortical brain function**—The loss of bodily functions along with brain damage possibly affecting personality, language skills, vision, memory, and actual physical movements; you may have capacity.

- **Loss of cortical brain function**—Varying degrees of damage to the brain, which could affect personality, language skills, vision, memory, and actual physical movements; you may have capacity.

- **Loss of brain stem function**—Requirement that basic bodily functions be supported mechanically; you may have capacity.

- **Loss of will to live**—The loss of desire to live, whether death is imminent or not.

Each of the preceding points of death is dramatically different. Add to the mix whether you have capacity. Consider each. If you have no capacity, do you want life-sustaining treatments if you've lost brain stem function? If you have capacity but need a machine to help you breathe, is that what you want? What about if you require feeding and fluids because you can't swallow or walk, but otherwise have capacity? There are many contingencies and possibilities. Consider each and what you truly want. Then communicate your wishes in your Living Will.

As we wrote this book, we talked a lot about the different points of death and their relationships to end-of-life decision making. One of the issues we struggled with the most was the perception of many individuals that refusing medical care was a form of suicide or that the physician following a patient's request was engaging in a form of euthanasia. Clearly, just the mention of suicide and euthanasia stirs up all sorts of feelings—emotional anxiety, political outrage, or moral questioning. We'll address them here in an effort to remove misunderstandings associated with these issues.

Euthanasia, generally, is defined as an action or inaction of a health care provider allowing a patient to die. In other words, euthanasia can be active or passive. Active euthanasia refers to a physician painlessly putting to death someone suffering from an incurable disease or condition. Passive euthanasia, on the other hand, is any act that allows a patient to die. Euthanasia can also be voluntary, nonvoluntary, or involuntary. Voluntary euthanasia occurs at the request of a conscious-with-capacity patient, or the patient's health care representative, who has received full information and has consented to the euthanasia. Nonvoluntary euthanasia takes place without the informed consent and request of a conscious-with-capacity patient or that patient's health care representative. The last type of euthanasia is involuntary euthanasia, which occurs over the objection of the patient or the patient's health care representative. Involuntary euthanasia is considered murder. Currently, Oregon, with its "Death with Dignity" law, is the only state that allows individuals to request active euthanasia.

Terminally ill patients who are in extreme pain may receive enough pain medication to induce a deep sleep to eliminate the pain. This is considered by most to be a palliation of the pain, not a form of euthanasia. You may have also heard of "mercy killings." Generally, this is a type of euthanasia by someone other than a doctor, such as a parent or child, who acts to end their loved one's suffering.

Suicide is taking one's own life intentionally and voluntarily. **Physician-assisted suicide** is when a doctor enables a terminally ill patient to take his or her own life. Suicide, in other words, is the act of the patient, not the provider.

Other than explaining euthanasia and suicide, we take no position on the subject in this book, with two exceptions. One, we firmly believe that the refusal of medical care, the implementation of a DNR, or following a Living Will is not suicide. Second, we strongly believe that any decision you make is your decision. We do not judge our clients' and patients' decisions. We support them within the confines of the law—regardless of their decisions. We support your decisions in the same way.

A Guide to Do Not Resuscitate (DNR) Orders

Over the years, we've heard many healthy clients, patients, and friends say, "I'm DNR," or "I've written my own DNR order." These, quite simply, are misstatements. That's why we want to begin by clearing up a big misconception regarding Do Not Resuscitate, or DNR, orders. Patients do not initiate or write DNR orders. These orders might be requested or suggested by a patient or even a nurse, but they can only be written and implemented by a properly licensed physician.

A DNR order originally directed that no extraordinary life-saving means be used: no chest compressions, no electric shocks, and no ventilator. Today, DNR orders can be tailored, with the assistance of your physician, to reflect your wishes. We suggest using the treatment table in Chapter 7, "Medical-Legal Wants: Understanding Interventions," to record your thoughts. Some individuals request that only chemical, or pharmaceutical, resuscitation be used. Others request all forms of life-saving measures, with the exception of a ventilator. Only you can decide this in consultation with your caregiver and with consideration given to all your conditions. You may also want to talk to your philosophical, religious, and spiritual advisors.

As we've noted throughout this chapter, just saying, "I don't want to be resuscitated," doesn't really work. And, in some extreme cases, failing to consider everything can cause you to end up in the very situation you're trying to avoid. We'll give you a brief example by telling you about Michael. He was done. Michael had lost his will to live. He decided that he wanted to cease all medical treatment, not just life support. So he refused additional medical care and stopped taking all his medication, although his physicians strongly advised against this. Rather than losing his life, Michael suffered a massive stroke when he stopped taking his blood pressure medicine. His body continued to function, but he lost most cerebral function. He lost his capacity and his ability to make his own decisions—everything he was trying to avoid.

A DNR order is extremely complex, but in certain situations, it may be warranted. Examples include a patient suffering from end stage kidney disease who no longer wants to receive dialysis; a patient with a progressive malignancy who has made the decision not to fight the cancer anymore; a patient with end-stage emphysema or end state COPD (chronic obstructive pulmonary disease) who, if he or she goes on a ventilator, will never be removed; or a patient with a blood disorder and progressive anemia where death is inevitable.

With that said, requesting that your doctor prepare a DNR order does not mean that you're refusing all medical care—you're simply requesting that you not be resuscitated in the event you stop breathing or your heart stops beating. Even if a DNR order is in place, you'll continue to receive pain medication and treatment of underlying infections and any other condition.

We recognize that these are extremely emotional, complex, and challenging issues. There is no right, wrong, or easy answer. The only correct decision is the decision that reflects your wants, wishes, and wills.

Medical-Legal Wishes

- Understand medical capacity and comas.
- Review the different points of death.
- Decide what the end of life means to you in each circumstance.
- Recognize what a DNR order means and discuss it with your providers.

9

Medical-Legal Wills:
Directives, Definitions,
and Discussions

If you were hooked up to a machine because you couldn't breathe on your own, and you had no hope of recovering, would you want to keep living? It's a terrible scenario to envision, but it *could* happen. And if it did, you'd want to be sure that your wishes were known and carried out. Even Kramer from *Seinfeld* understood the importance of a trustworthy person to represent him. In one episode, after asking Elaine to be the one to "pull the plug," Kramer announced that he wanted "someone tough" to make the hard decisions. Although we chuckled at Kramer's antics, his thought process was nothing to laugh at: Determining your wants and wishes at the end of life and choosing the right individual to make your decisions—medical and financial—are critical for ensuring that your will is carried out.

Real life, though, is no TV show. Decisions to be made aren't clear-cut. But before reviewing the different documents you should consider, let's talk about who you want to make your decisions if you're unable to make them yourself. First, you'll need to name an individual (or more than one individual) to act as your **agent** (also called an **attorney-in-fact**). This person would be able to make all financial and business decisions for you under a Power of Attorney. Second, you'll need to appoint one or more health care representatives who would make all medical and mental health care decisions on your behalf under a Health Care Proxy. He or she would talk to your doctors, review your medical records, and consent to or refuse medical procedures, for example.

Who's Who?

Principal—The individual signing the Power of Attorney or Health Care Proxy and asking an agent or health care representative to make decisions on his or her behalf—in other words, you!

Agent—The individual or individuals named to make your financial and business decisions under a Power of Attorney. Also called an attorney-in-fact.

Health care representative—The individual or individuals named to make your health care and medical decisions under a Health Care Proxy.

With this in mind, for some of you, your spouse may be the logical choice to take on one or both of these roles. But for others, a spouse isn't the best person to elect because of the emotions related to such decisions, the age or health of your mate, or the current state of your relationship. For those of you who aren't married, do you pick the sibling you haven't seen in five years or your best friend who lives around the corner?

When making this crucial choice, it's important not to be swayed by family pressures or social conventions. Instead, study your friends and family, and then decide who is most likely to make similar decisions and respect your wishes. Use common sense. Follow your gut instinct. Of equal importance, ask yourself who's smart enough to ask for help from appropriate sources. You don't always need a Wall Street guru to manage your financial affairs, but you do need someone who is wise enough to seek counsel before making investments. You also don't need to name your third cousin once removed simply because he's the only doctor in the family. Instead, pick an individual who can be trusted to follow your wishes regarding end-of-life care and, as Kramer said, can make the "tough" medical decisions. If you're unsure about this person now, he or she isn't the right individual to make decisions for you at any time. If you're concerned about upsetting someone with your decision, leave a letter explaining your rationale in picking a particular child over another. We understand that this is an extremely difficult and often gut-wrenching determination, but you must make a decision. Failing to decide who will make your decisions results in difficulties for all involved, and it almost guarantees that your wishes will *not* be carried out.

Health Care Documents 101

Living Will—A legal document that outlines your wishes regarding your medical care at the end of life, including treatments you want or don't want. Also called an **Advance Directive for Health Care—Instruction Directive**, **Medical Directive**, or **Directive to Physicians**.

Health Care Proxy—A legal document that appoints an individual, your health care representative, to make your medical decisions for you if you're unable. Also called a **Durable Power of Attorney for Health Care**, **Advance Directive for Health Care—Proxy Directive**, **Medical Power of Attorney**, and **Advance Directive for Health Care**.

These can be two separate documents or combined into one document. The combination document is cumulatively called an **Advance Directive** or **Health Care Advance Directive**.

We can't emphasize enough the importance of having a Living Will, Health Care Proxy, and Power of Attorney. We agree with Abigail, age 42, who said:

> *Failing to plan is planning to fail.... I want my wishes carried out, so I've planned ahead and selected the individuals to act on my behalf.*

Identifying the individuals to act for you and putting it in writing can also remove any family disputes over your care and your intentions. Wendy, age 31, a registered nurse, has seen many situations in which a family bickered over the next medical steps to take until the Health Care Proxy was located and "resolved any disputes over who should be making the decisions."

What If I Don't Have a Health Care Proxy?

Certain states have statutes or administrative codes that determine who acts on your behalf if you haven't designated a health care representative. Others do not. Regardless, why let your state or someone else decide who makes your medical decisions when you can decide yourself today?

There are some important points to remember in selecting your agents and health care representatives. First, your agent and health care representative do not have to be the same person. Second, in addition to your primary agent or health care representative, you should always select one or two successors in case the designated individual dies before you, is unavailable, or is otherwise unable to fulfill his or her duty. Some individuals choose to name multiple agents and health care representatives—for example, two children or a spouse and a child. You can then determine whether they can act individually or if you want them to act unanimously. If you choose more than one individual and you're unsure whether your selected decision makers can work together, some practitioners suggest including an "arbitration clause" in your documents, which outlines a means to resolve disputes. Our feeling is that if you think your agents and health care representatives can't work harmoniously, select someone else. In the event of a crisis, you don't want your agents or health care representatives running to an arbitration panel or the courts to decide what happens next.

What About Your Old Health Care Proxy and Living Will?

When you sign new documents, be sure that a statement is included revoking all prior instruments. If you have copies of the old documents, destroy them by burning, ripping, or writing "Revoked" in clear handwriting across the first page. If copies of the old documents have been distributed, collect them or ask the individuals holding the old documents to destroy them for you.

With this background, we'll talk about each document. Then we'll discuss the importance of talking to the individuals you named in each document to emphasize your wants, wishes, and wills.

A Guide to Health Care Proxies and Living Wills

The unfortunate case of Terry Schiavo brought to the forefront the importance of Health Care Proxies and Living Wills. Deciding today, while you're able, who should make your medical decisions if you're unable and what medical care you want at the end of life is critical. Individuals are passionate about these determinations, even making it clear in unconventional ways that they don't want to be kept alive in certain circumstances. One 80-year old woman in Iowa went so far as to have "Do Not Resuscitate" tattooed on her chest. Others joke about simplifying Living Wills.

The New Living Will

Under no circumstances should my fate be put in the hands of pin-head politicians who couldn't pass ninth-grade biology if their lives depended on it or lawyers/doctors interested in simply running up the bills. If a reasonable amount of time passes and I fail to ask for at least one of the following

- Glass of wine
- Margarita
- Martini
- Cold beer
- Chicken fried steak and cream gravy
- Mexican food
- French fries
- Pizza
- Bowl of ice cream
- Chocolate
- Sex

it should be presumed that I will never get better. When such a determination is reached, I hereby instruct my appointed person and attending physicians to pull the plug, reel in the tubes, and call it a day.

Courtesy of an Internet chain e-mail.

If only Living Wills could be this simple!

Health care documents can be confusing, especially because they can be completed in a number of ways. The Health Care Proxy, Durable Power of Attorney for Health Care, Medical Power of Attorney, and Advance Directive for Health Care—Proxy Directive (we refer to them as a Health Care Proxy) all appoint an individual to act on your behalf. The Living Will and Advance Directive for Health Care—Instruction Directive state your wishes at the end of life (we refer to them as a Living Will). Often there are two separate documents, but they may be combined into a single legal document simply called an Advance Directive. You can have a Health Care Proxy without a Living Will, and vice versa, although a Living Will without someone to make your wishes happen may not be particularly helpful.

Before we discuss Living Wills, we need to consider who, if necessary, will implement your Living Will. It's your health care representative (the individual named under your Health Care Proxy) who makes your medical decisions for you, but only if you're unable to do so yourself. As long as you have the capacity and consciousness to make decisions, you remain in charge of your medical care. So why do you need to designate a health care representative? Because there are many moments, even during routine medical procedures, that you may lack decision-making capacity. You could be under anesthesia, suffering from temporary drug-induced confusion, or on narcotic painkillers that cloud your judgment. No matter what the cause of your inability to act, you want your health care providers to know who makes your decisions and whom they may talk to about your situation.

Thanks to **HIPAA** (the Health Insurance Portability and Accountability Act of 1996) and its privacy rule, your health care provider can no longer reveal information to your "next of kin" gathered anxiously in the waiting area. HIPAA requires that your protected health information remain confidential unless you have authorized a health care representative or other individuals to hear such information. While this can be burdensome, in certain circumstances, it's beneficial. It prevents strangers or individuals with whom you no longer have a relationship (for example, a separated spouse or a child whom you haven't seen in 20 years) from learning your condition and attempting to make decisions for you. It also allows you the opportunity to specifically name the person you want to make those calls—your life partner, best friend, or other nonrelative who traditionally would have no "next of kin" rights to act on your behalf—with your blessing.

Who Can Know Your Health Care Status?

The folks who are legally allowed to learn all about what ails you are limited by HIPAA. First, it's your health care representative who you've named in your Health Care Proxy. You can also give your physician a list of other people he or she can talk to. Why do you want these people to know your health care status? Maybe you have trouble hearing. Or maybe you're feeling so sick that you want someone else to get information for you. Just be sure to keep the list up-to-date. Although these folks can know about your situation, only your health care representative can make decisions for you. Use the following chart to make sure your provider has the 4-1-1 on the people you've picked to know all about you:

My Who-Can-Know-What Chart

Name	SSN	Address	Phone Numbers	Relationship to Patient	Limits on Information Provided
1.					
2.					
3.					
4.					
5.					

Along with stating *who* may act on your behalf, you may also include in your Health Care Proxy *what* acts your health care representative may undertake for you. For example, you may want to specifically outline that your health care representative may speak with your physicians, direct what medical care you may or may not receive, and determine the best level of care if you suffer from an acute, chronic, mental, or terminal illness and need nursing or other long-term care. These are issues that should be discussed and addressed with your attorney and may be dependent upon the state in which you reside.

The companion document is the Living Will, also known as an Advanced Directive for Health Care—Instruction Directive. Your Living Will is your written directive to your health care representative and your physicians regarding your intentions at the end of your life. It usually states that you intend that no life-prolonging treatment be sought or continued if you're terminally ill, injured, permanently unconscious, or otherwise unlikely to survive. In other words, Living Wills state in writing, in a format dictated by the state in which you are residing, that you specifically request certain treatments not be continued if you're in one of a number of conditions. In your Living Will, you should specifically list the treatments you don't want to receive (for example, cardiopulmonary resuscitation, ventilation, and feeding tubes and fluids), as well as those you wish to receive (for example, pain medication). The Living Will may also include a statement regarding organ donation or your intentions if you're pregnant. A Living Will should not be confused with a Do Not Resuscitate, or DNR, order. Remember, a DNR order can be issued only by a licensed physician, often after consultation with the patient or the patient's health care representative and with consideration given to the patient's Living Will, if any. It's important to note that the final decision remains yours, so long as you're able to make such decisions. If you're unable, the decision belongs to your health care representative with due regard to your wishes as outlined in your Living Will.

Your Living Will shouldn't be a form you've printed off the Internet or a boilerplate document given to you by the staff of the local hospital when you're being admitted. Your Living Will should reflect your health and circumstances, your wants and wishes, as well as your values and beliefs. Although considering this subject isn't easy, we believe doing so provides an opportunity for you to create a directive that truly reflects your wants. And because we all have different desires and different situations, a standard form just won't work.

What Are Life-Sustaining Treatments?

In a Living Will, you may state that certain life-sustaining treatments be stopped or never started. But what exactly are they? We discussed them earlier, but we thought a recap of the most common treatments would be helpful:

- **Cardiopulmonary resuscitation** (CPR) is a combination of rescue breathing and chest compressions delivered to patients when their heart is thought to stop beating (cardiac arrest). CPR can support a small amount of blood flow to the heart and brain to "buy time" if normal heart function can be restored.

- **Respiratory support** is the administration of extra oxygen through various mechanisms such as **high flow oxygen therapy** (oxygen given by face mask or nasal prongs or cannulas), **continuous positive airways pressure** (forcing oxygen into areas of the lungs being underutilized), **endotracheal intubation and ventilation** (putting a tube into the mouth or nose of a person who cannot breathe on his or her own and having a machine breathe for the person), or a **tracheotomy** (a surgical incision in the windpipe).

- **Artificially administered feeding and fluids** are provided to a person who cannot eat or drink on his or her own. There are several types of artificial feeding and fluids: **total enteral nutrition** (using the intestinal tract to eat) through the use of a **nasogastric tube** (a feeding tube temporarily placed through a person's nose down to his or her stomach for liquefied food to be pumped) or a **gastric** (or **duodenal** or **jejunal**) tube (a feeding tube that is placed through the stomach or small intestine wall and out through the skin of the abdomen) and **total parenteral nutrition** (providing nutrition by going around the intestinal tract using intravenous (IV) fluids or a larger venous catheter in a vein).

- **Defibrillation** is a process in which an electronic device gives an electric shock to the heart to reestablish normal contraction rhythms in a heart having dangerous abnormal beats (**arrhythmia**) or in cardiac arrest.
- **Surgery** is any invasive procedure or operation. Surgery may be minimal (such as the placement of a central line for IV access), major (such as open heart surgery), or somewhere in between.
- **Antibiotics** are drugs designed to fight infections. They may be administered by mouth (PO), by the vein (IV), or by a feeding tube.

Clearly, we don't know today what medical treatments will be available 5, 10, or 15 years from now. As such, a Living Will is a directive, not a mandate, and asks that the decision maker consider your thoughts and desires as well as current circumstances. In most situations, it clarifies your intent and makes it easier for your health care representative to take the necessary actions to fulfill your wishes. For Claudia, age 48, her mother's Living Will and Health Care Proxy proved invaluable because they allowed her, as health care representative, to request the termination of life support after her mother had slipped into a coma. Without it, her mother could have lingered, hooked to a ventilator with no likelihood of regaining consciousness, for who knows how long—something Claudia's mother vehemently opposed. The desires of individuals at the end of life, or victims of tragic injuries, are so important that the U.S. Army is examining whether battlefield doctors should have access to soldiers' Living Wills. Without access to an injured serviceperson's wishes, extraordinary measures are taken to save lives, even though it was a soldier's wish not to be kept alive with severe brain damage.

Does a Living Will Mean I Want Euthanasia?

No. Euthanasia is an active or passive act to end your life by another—for example, providing a drug overdose or actively seeking a lethal injection or not providing a treatment. Refusing medical care at the end of life when there is no likelihood of recovery is *not* generally considered euthanasia or suicide. If you're concerned about this distinction, talk with your spiritual advisor because opinions differ as to how much intervention a patient should request.

In your Living Will, specificity is of paramount importance. A simple statement of "no heroic measures" is useless. What's a "heroic measure?" The definition of heroic is "exhibiting or marked by courage or daring." Clearly, that's not a very helpful statement to a health care provider. This is why you should avoid simple one-page Living Wills (usually based on a state's original legislative language) found on the Internet or in stationary shops. We know they come from the statutes of the various states, but these forms are merely the starting point for your decision making. You need to specify exactly what type of medical care you want to receive and the circumstances under which such care should be refused. Your personalized Living Will should mirror the statutory language of the state in which you live to be sure it's effective under local law—another reason talking to a lawyer is better than just picking up a one-size-fits-all legal form. You should also include a statement that your health care providers won't be sued for following your wishes.

If you're religious, be sure to ask your attorney to include in your health care documents language reflecting your particular religious beliefs. The Roman Catholic Church recommends specific language to be added to a Living Will that requests that the Sacraments of Reconciliation and Anointing of the Sick and Viaticum be provided, as well as a statement regarding the Catholic definition of life. Check with your parish or diocese for this language. If you're Jewish, talk to your rabbi because different branches within the Jewish religion have different views, including the definition of death as it pertains to organ donation. The same considerations exist for Muslims. Again, your cleric or an Islamic scholar will be able to assist you in including language that reflects Islamic law. Protestants have no clear guidelines, although various denominations may provide suggested language.

In Chapter 8, "Medical-Legal Wishes: Defining Capacity, Consciousness, and Contingencies," we discussed the different, defined points of death. Which definition meets your view? Be sure to include that definition in your Living Will. If you're suffering from advanced dementia and are otherwise healthy, do you want to refuse all further health care? If the use of a ventilator or respirator for a brief period of time during a chronic illness could return you to an active and healthy lifestyle, do you want to emphatically refuse such treatment? If you're adamant that you do not want to receive artificially administered nutrition and hydration, this should be spelled out and highlighted in your Living Will. Are you concerned about pain? If so, ask your lawyer to include that you want to receive pain medication, even if this medication will shorten your life expectancy. The following outlines some of the issues to consider:

- State the circumstances in which your Living Will should become effective, such as if you've received a terminal prognosis, you're in a persistent vegetative state with irreversible brain damage, in an irreversible coma, suffering from irreversible advanced dementia, or there is no expectation of recovery.

- When the circumstances that you've outlined exist, list with specificity the medical care you no longer want to receive (such as cardiopulmonary resuscitation, respiratory assistance, and therapeutic treatments).

- Make a specific statement that you want to refuse or receive intravenous feeding and fluids.

- Avoid general or vague statements such as "heroic measures" or "extraordinary means."

- If desired, include a request that you want to be an organ donor, if feasible, and that all steps should be taken to make your organs available. Today, almost everyone can be an organ donor. The organ transplant team will decide at the time whether your organs can be used.

- Include a statement in the event you are pregnant. For example, you could choose to be kept alive as a human incubator if a child will be born, regardless of the child's prognosis, or only if a medical certainty exists that a nondisabled child will be born. Alternatively, you can request that your Living Will be given full force and effect whether or not you're expecting—in other words you won't be kept alive just because you're pregnant.

A Living Will doesn't necessarily have to be a document refusing medical care. It can also state that your physicians and your health care representative take all actions necessary to prolong your life. Again, the goal is to provide your decision maker and your caregivers with a clear, written directive of your intentions regarding your medical care. There would likely not have been such protracted legal battles between Terry Schiavo's husband and family if Terry at least had a Living Will that clearly stated her wishes. A Living Will could prevent your loved ones from struggling with the same issues. Make sure that you or your health care representative discusses the specifics of your Living Will with your providers. It should be placed on any hospital chart. Make sure it's there every time you're hospitalized.

A Guide to Powers of Attorney

A Power of Attorney is the document you've probably heard of the most. Chances are, some of you have already signed one, maybe when closing on a house or to allow a spouse to conduct banking transactions for you. Generally, there are three types of Powers of Attorney: General, Limited, and Springing. Both the General and Limited Powers of Attorney are active upon signing, which means that you do not have to be incapacitated or unable to act at such time as your agent under the Power of Attorney seeks to act. This makes many individuals uncomfortable—do I really want someone to have the power to act while I'm fine? As noted earlier, if you can't trust this individual now, he or she should not act as your agent either now or in the future. Period.

Appointing someone to act as your agent is not to be taken lightly. So why do it? Because there may come a time, during a difficult illness or other incapacity, that you lack the ability to make financial decisions for yourself. Or you could be hit by a bus tomorrow and end up in a coma. Either way, you'll need assistance writing checks, paying bills, filing your taxes, and making other financial decisions, either day-to-day or long-term. John, a 46-year-old financial advisor, agrees, commenting that Powers of Attorney are both "valuable and necessary." Without appointing someone to make these decisions *now*—while you're still able—your family and friends could be forced to request court involvement to adjudicate the appropriate person or persons to act for you.

If you were to become incapacitated without having a valid Power of Attorney, the courts could appoint a guardian to act on your behalf. This guardian would control your finances and could make all health care decisions on your behalf. Alternatively, a court might appoint a conservator to handle your finances only. Each state has different definitions of the role of a guardian or conservator. Regardless, if there is a court action, a *guardian ad litem* would likely be appointed on your behalf. This is different from a guardian. (Don't you love the law making everything so incredibly confusing?) The *guardian ad litem*'s job is to make sure that you really are incapacitated and that the appointment of a guardian or conservator is the best thing for you. As part of the process, your medical conditions, as well as your assets, would become a matter of public record. These can be both time-consuming and costly proceedings. Because there may come a time that you need assistance, you should be the one to select the individual or individuals to act on your behalf. We cannot stress enough the necessity of having a Power of Attorney, especially if you've recently received a less-than-favorable prognosis.

The distinction between the General and Limited Power of Attorney is the breadth of the powers that you give to your agent. A General Power of Attorney is nearly limitless, allowing your agent to do everything you could do, including selling real estate and personal property, creating trusts, resigning appointments, entering safe deposit boxes, and making gifts, for example. As noted earlier, a Power of Attorney is for financial and business decisions only.

What Exactly Is a General Durable Power of Attorney?

When you sign a Power of Attorney, you give your agent the powers authorized by law in the state in which you reside as well as a general power to act in all ways that you would act, which could include the power to

- Conduct all banking transactions, including depositing and withdrawing funds and making electronic or wire transfers
- Open, close, and maintain bank, brokerage, or other accounts
- Buy and sell securities of any kind
- Open, close, and enter safe deposit boxes
- Spend funds on behalf of dependents
- Loan or borrow funds and collect debts
- Collect funds, including interest and dividends
- Vote Proxies
- Purchase and dispose of real and personal property
- Make gifts

- Create, revoke, or amend trust agreements
- Prepare and file tax returns
- Change beneficiary forms
- Resign or renounce appointments, disclaim interests in property, hire persons, or engage services of any kind

A Limited Power of Attorney specifies that only certain, particular acts can be performed by your agent, such as writing checks, making bank deposits, and paying taxes. We believe the General Power of Attorney is best, provided you have a trusted individual to act as your agent, because if you need assistance, why limit the help your agent can give you? If you're still concerned, talk to your attorney about the best alternative for you given your particular circumstances.

Both the General and Limited Power of Attorney should be "durable." In other words, the document should specifically state that the Power of Attorney will remain valid even when you become incapacitated or unable to act. Without this, it could be argued that the document ceases to be effective upon such an event—something you're trying to avoid. Check with your counselor to be sure that your current or any future documents are, in fact, durable.

The third type of Power of Attorney is a Springing Power of Attorney, which only takes effect when you're incapacitated. Although many think this is the perfect solution, and it may be for some, it often defeats the purpose of executing a Power of Attorney. If the document states that it's only effective on your inability to act, your agent must now prove to a bank or brokerage firm, for example, that you are, in fact, incapacitated. This may mean, at the very least, provision of doctors' notes or medical reports. Time and energy are now wasted trying to prove that you're no longer able to act. It's likely that many institutions will not honor such a Power of Attorney. (We've seen it often.) As such, we have serious concerns regarding such springing documents.

With that said, you should discuss any apprehensions with your lawyer. Let him or her know exactly what powers you want your agent to have and any other issues that worry you. If you're nervous about providing a fully active Power of Attorney to your agent at this time, your counselor may be able to help you. Some attorneys will hold all of the signed documents in their files pursuant to a **Holding Letter**, in which you ask your attorney to keep the original documents in his or her file until such time as the agent provides evidence of your incapacity to your lawyer.

The Documents Are Signed. What Now?

First, we suggest signing at least four duplicate originals of your Health Care Proxy, Living Will, and Power of Attorney. Keep one duplicate original of each document with your lawyer. Originals can be lost or destroyed, and this will ensure that at least one original remains safe. Next, communicate to your named representatives where the other original documents are located. We recommend leaving documents in a readily accessible location such as an unlocked fire box or designated "important paper drawer" in a desk or bureau. We do not suggest safe deposit boxes because your loved ones trying to access the box may not have signing authority, or the bank may be closed for several days due to a weekend or holiday. In the event of a medical emergency, you want your representative to have immediate access to the necessary documents. In addition, you should tell your primary care physician that you have signed the documents and ask if he or she would like a copy. When admitted to a hospital, bring along a copy yourself. Last but not least, hold onto the original documents. Allow institutions and providers to make copies but ask that the originals be returned to you. The reason is simple: If you give all of your originals away and subsequently become incapacitated and unable to sign new documents, it's as if you never went to the trouble of signing the documents in the first place. Check with your attorney to see if he or she has additional suggestions.

A Guide to Communicating Your Health Care Wants and Wishes

Documents are critical components of ordering your affairs. We believe that communicating your wants and wishes to your family and friends is of equal importance.

We've witnessed such conversations, which sometimes include a great deal of humor. Take Betty, age 42, recently diagnosed with cancer. She told her sister, after she signed her Health Care Proxy and her Living Will, that she wanted her to do everything possible to keep her alive. "Don't pull the plug," she mandated, "unless I've lost a limb; then go ahead. I'm too superficial to live without all of my external parts." We agree, Betty's wish is a little superficial. But it's what she wants. She took the time to clearly communicate her wishes, not just in writing, but in a conversational statement that made it clear to her sister exactly how she feels.

We acknowledge that these are incredibly difficult issues to discuss. We can't tell you the number of people who refused to complete our simple survey on the subject because it was "too emotional," "too morbid," or "too sad." That's part of why we've written this book: to provide a catalyst to discuss these subjects. We encourage you to have a heart-to-heart with your agents, health care representatives, and health care providers. Tell them exactly how you feel. Be specific. Continue the dialogue over time, and be sure each individual truly understands. Sophia, age 77, has a Living Will, but she has also made it emphatically clear to her husband and sons that she dreads a long, lingering illness and "wants the opportunity for a quick death." As Sophia's husband noted, "she is unyielding on this point, and we understand her wishes."

Harold Ivan Smith, in his book *Finding Your Way to Say Goodbye*, emphasizes the importance of clearly stating your wishes and also doing so in writing:

Words written on a paper are like money in escrow. Putting your wishes into writing is a gift to your family. Too many families get 'ambushed' in hospital corridors and family lounges because the patient did not clearly verbalize wishes and did not dialogue with loved ones about those wishes.

Make sure this doesn't happen to your loved ones.

It's also important to recognize the horribly painful and emotional decision that you're asking your health care representative to make. When 40-year-old Cindy's aunt was dying of liver failure, her brother was charged with making decisions on their aunt's behalf; it was "a really difficult, life-changing, family-tearing time for him." Virginia Morris writes in *Talking About Death Won't Kill You*:

Think not just about safe, sterile subjects like the medicine and legalities and ethics involved, but about death, the big picture. Death with a capital D. Because when you sign a living will or make a promise to a loved one, you're not talking simply about using a medical procedure or refusing it. You're talking about finality. About mortality. About pain and disease and decline and final good-byes. It is easy to say, "I would never want that procedure," but have you tried to put yourself inside the mind of a dying person? Have you ever really imagined what it is like to make life-and death decisions for someone whom you can't live without?

Have a family meeting to discuss your views. Let your health care representative know that he or she shouldn't feel guilty for carrying out your wishes. Assure this person that making the "tough" decision is the ultimate act of love. And keep telling him or her that.

Jamie, age 58, understands how difficult it is to fulfill the wishes of loved ones:

You just have to be strong enough to abide by their wishes. It would have been easier if I'd been making the decision for myself. My parents were wonderful people, I never saw them do anything wrong, they took care of me as a child and protected me from harm. How do you say 'yes' to turning off life support? It was the hardest decision I ever made in my life, and if I knew it would be my decision, I would have discussed it more with them.

Despite being a nurse, Elise, age 42, struggled when faced with a similar decision:

For many years I thought I 'knew' what I would do if faced with that situation and then suddenly when it was right in front of me with someone I was close to, my emotions really took over, and I struggled to figure out what the right thing was to do.

It's never easy.

We've all heard the anguished stories of final days: Loved ones placed on respirators, kept alive by artificial means, or given unwanted food and nutrition. People often place blame on the hospital, nurses, or doctors. We believe this blame is misplaced. Physicians, health care providers, and emergency personnel are trained to save lives. It's their job. It's the responsibility of you, or your health care representative, to refuse medical care. You or your representative must be proactive. If 9-1-1 is called to the home of a terminal cancer patient, the paramedics will perform all acts necessary to resuscitate. In a moment of crisis, a health care provider will not waste time looking through a chart to determine if the patient has a Living Will and then read through several pages of "legalese" to determine what to do next. If it's what you want, request a Do Not Resuscitate order if hospitalized and the end of life is imminent (see Chapter 8). Don't request emergency care. There are options. Discuss them with your physician to determine how best to act.

You need your health care representative to fight for you, to refuse unwanted medical procedures, and, perhaps, to make a determination that ends your life. You need someone strong, someone who will make the decisions you want, and someone who is able to set aside his or her emotions and step into your shoes. Or if you want every possible action taken to keep you alive, you want someone who is willing to fight your insurance company, request alternative and perhaps unorthodox treatments, and to find the next best course of treatment given your situation.

How Often Should I Update My Documents?

We suggest that you review your documents at least every five years or whenever you have a major life-changing event—the death of a named agent or representative or a change in your health, such as a diagnosis of cancer or the beginning stages of Alzheimer's disease.

We're sure that you've sensed the overriding theme of this chapter: You have the power to decide who will and who will not act on your behalf, as well as what level of care is right for you. They're important decisions. And they're *your* decisions. Remember, don't be concerned about what others will think or if feelings will be hurt. You need to think of yourself, your affairs, and your care and not be concerned with anyone else. In the final analysis, you need to do what's right for you. We know it's difficult, and we wish we could work with each one of you. Just be comforted that in deciding who will act on your behalf, you'll make it easier on your family and friends and ultimately on yourself.

Medical-Legal Wills

- Prepare a Health Care Proxy.
- Prepare a Living Will—add additional instructions important to you.

- Prepare your Who-Can-Know-What chart.

- Share your Health Care Proxy, Living Will, and Who-Can-Know-What chart with all of your providers.

- Prepare a Power of Attorney.

- Communicate your wants, wishes, and wills with your family, friends, agents, health care representatives, and providers.

Section IV

The Wants, Wishes, and Wills of Your Selfless Contributions

We want to begin Section IV by saying "Thank you." Thank you just for thinking about participating in clinical trials and studies that further health care discoveries every day. And thank you for donating your time and energy to the many worthy causes that work toward finding disease cures and preventing disease in the future. We admire your dedication, diligence, and desire to make a difference. Thank you if you've said "yes" to potentially becoming an organ donor.

We think of Section IV as the story of the modern-day Good Samaritan who gives back to the community by giving, literally, of him- or herself. Although we also applaud monetary charitable gifts, which we'll talk more about in Chapter 14, "Estate Planning Wishes: Caring for Family, Friends, and Foundations," selfless contributions of organs, cells, and information are invaluable. These are gifts—such as a pint of blood at your local blood drive—that can be given today with immediate benefit. They can also be donations that assist in long-term efforts to understand a particular disease (such as a tissue donation to a research institute) or the act of sharing your personal information for complex studies.

Throughout this section, we tell you about donation and research communities, as well as patient advocacy groups. We also explain how you can define your donation goals, protect yourself from liability as a volunteer, and make your volunteer experience the best that it can be. Lastly, we'll explain more about informed consent, record keeping and reporting, and who actually owns what you've been kind enough to donate.

Your selfless contributions are a true example of exercising your free will to help others. And, as we said earlier, we applaud your efforts.

10

Selfless Contribution Wants: Donating Time, Tissue, and Treatment Data

Since we both were young, we've been dedicated volunteers, assisting in local community events through our scout troops and continuing our efforts through college and beyond. As we've gotten older, what has amazed us the most are the countless opportunities to give, as well as the generosity of others. With so many opportunities, the hardest thing, we've discovered, is deciding just what to do.

A Guide to Patient Advocacy Communities

Patient advocacy groups exist in almost every size community in America. We think of them as organizations of concerned and knowledgeable individuals with the means and abilities to do something about a particular issue. The groups needing your attention aren't limited to large organizations. Some of today's modern charities are small and dedicated to particular needs in your community or the ravages of a specific disease. The goal of each organization is to fulfill a need not currently being met by governments, providers, or currently existing charities. And they're looking both to help you and to be helped by you.

Many of these organizations are dedicated to finding cures for specific diseases or offering information and medical attention in times of crisis. Thanks to Clara Barton, the U.S. Congress gave the Red Cross a federal charter in 1881. (It began in Europe in 1864.) Not only is the Red Cross a disaster relief organization, it's the biggest blood bank in our country. The first disease-specific charity was the March of Dimes, which began in 1938 with a mission to cure polio. Today, it fights to find cures for birth defects. In 1946, UNICEF was started by the United Nations to provide health care, clothing, and food to European children facing disease and famine.

You may recognize names like the American Cancer Society and the Leukemia/Lymphoma Society, but perhaps you've never heard of Project ALS. Each organization has a different mission and goal. The American Cancer Society not only raises money to research cures, but it's also extremely active in cancer prevention, such as recommending colon cancer screenings for everyone over the age of 50. The Leukemia/Lymphoma Society, on the other hand, focuses primarily on research. Then there's Project ALS, which fights what's more commonly known as Lou Gehrig's disease. Jennifer Estess, the brave, young woman who started Project ALS, worked vigilantly to find a cure until her own death from ALS in 2003. Her fight continues today.

The opportunities to give of yourself are infinite. What these groups need most from you is your time and energy. They also need your expertise on everything from maintaining their headquarters to research to fundraising. Look to each organization and group and find out what it really does and what help it needs. If you're more interested in finding disease cures, focus your efforts on research organizations. Do you want to help individuals currently suffering from disease? Support a local chapter that provides transportation services to chemotherapy patients or meals to infectious disease sufferers. No matter what group it is that you support, your efforts will make a difference.

If you're looking into small, local organizations, make sure you do your due diligence before joining the volunteer ranks. Just because an organization is nonprofit doesn't mean there isn't a financial motive behind the organization. Look out for advocacy groups run by individuals who are also trying to "sell" you or someone else a particular product or service. Verify with the IRS (www.irs.gov) to be sure that the charity has nonprofit status. Although every organization begins with a noble purpose, even the most well-meaning individuals can be led astray.

At the same time, if you're currently ill, don't forget to ask what these organizations can do for you. Log on to the Web sites for the organizations dedicated to fighting your illness. Check with your health care provider for recommendations. Your provider should be able to give you information and resources at the very least.

A Guide to Donation Communities

If you renewed your driver's license recently, you were probably asked if you'd like to be an organ donor. Donations, however, aren't limited to organs. Every time you give a pint of blood, you've made a donation. Although the donation of an organ can mean the immediate difference between life and death, gifts of blood and tissue potentially have even longer-term benefits.

Organ Donations

The first donations were tissue, including blood. Thanks to Joseph Lister, antiseptic was discovered, which gave us sterile surgery environments. Anesthesia gave us the ability to put patients to sleep. Next, we learned more about the immune system of the body. This made organ donations possible. The first successful transplant was a cornea in 1905 in Olomouc, Czech Republic. Since then, we've seen successful organ transplants of kidneys in 1954 (Boston, Massachusetts and Paris, France), livers in 1963 (Denver, Colorado and Cambridge, England), a pancreas in 1966 (Minneapolis, Minnesota), a heart in 1967 (Cape Town, South Africa), bone marrow in 1968 (Madison, Wisconsin and Minneapolis, Minnesota), a lung in 1981 (Stanford, Connecticut), a hand in 1999 (Louisville, Kentucky), and even a face in 2005 (Amiens, France).

Our Favorite Bumper Sticker

Don't take your organs to heaven, heaven knows we need them here.

Why are organ donations so important? Transplants save lives and preserve limbs, the goal of every physician. They give chronically, and often terminally, ill patients a chance at life. Organ donations are run by groups at the state level. To find out more about the donation opportunities where you live, log onto http://organdonor.gov.

Blood Donations

If you've never given blood, we're sure that you know someone who has. There's been such great success with the collection and storage of blood that local blood drives are commonplace. We see people line up to give blood after tragedies like September 11. In addition to donating for others, you can make self-donations in anticipation of an upcoming surgery or to help family and friends. Keep in mind, though, that if you're making this type of donation, it takes three days to process blood. For this reason, a general blood donation may be better and will help not just you or your loved one, but everyone.

When you head to your local blood drive and sign up, you're giving a lot more than a pint of blood. You're actually giving

- **White blood cells**—These are generally not used.

- **Red blood cells**—This is what we think of most and, usually, why one receives a blood transfusion.

- **Platelets**—Platelets are cell products that circulate in your blood and are necessary for blood clotting and to reduce bleeding or bruising. It takes donations from five to eight people to have a single dose of transfusable platelets.

- **Plasma and coagulation factors**—These are critical components for people with liver dysfunction and may also help people with blood-clotting problems such as hemophilia. A common form is "FFP"—fresh, frozen plasma.

Adult stem cells may also be taken from blood and used in a transplant. They are *not* the stem cells in the news that come from embryos. Such donations are done only under special circumstances (such as to benefit a patient with certain leukemias, lymphomas, or primary bone marrow failure disorders).

Blood Donations 101

Blood donors must be healthy, at least 17 years old (16 in some states) and weigh 110 pounds or more. Eight weeks must have passed since you last gave blood. If you take certain medications, are anemic, have transmittable infectious diseases, or other health conditions, you can't give blood. To learn more about being a donor, ask your health care provider or log onto www.givelife.org.

Donated tissue can be used to search for common responses to medications. The goal is to determine what treatments will work for some patients and not for others. To learn more, log onto the Web site for The American Cancer Biorepository at http://theacb.com.

Bone Marrow

Bone marrow is a source of both red and white blood cells and is found in the soft, fatty vascular tissue that fills most bone cavities. Because bone marrow is so rich in blood cells, donations are extremely important to individuals suffering from certain diseases, most notably leukemia. Donations can be for yourself (**autograph**) or another (**allograph**). If you're making a donation for another, it can be for a specific person (in which case the donation would be immediate) or for the general population. A donation to the general public is made by becoming part of the national bone marrow registry. To become a member of the registry, you submit a sample and wait to make a donation until a match is made. Whether or not you're called is a matter of timing and matches. Bone marrow matches are determined on a six-point system. To date, most bone marrow donors have been Caucasian, leaving other racial groups underrepresented and in need of donors. Why does race make a difference? Because different races often have different bone marrow characteristics. If you're interested in becoming a donor, log onto the Bone Marrow Foundation site at www.bonemarrow.org.

Scientific Research

For some, the ultimate donation is a contribution of their body to scientific research on their passing. It's a generous, thoughtful, and important gift to the scientific community. There are many organizations accepting donations. If you're interested, check with your physician for suggestions in your community.

A Guide to Research Communities

If you're squeamish about needles or can't give blood, what can you do? You can share your personal information and protected health information. Information donation is critical material for researchers. Your information covers everything from your current condition to your complications to your outcome—and everything in between.

You can donate your information by participating in studies and trials. Studies are conducted every day on everything from sleep patterns to exercise habits to the effects of stress on health. The goal is to find out why a particular population or group of people does what they do or why this works and that doesn't.

Walk across any college campus, and we're sure you'll see solicitations to participate in trials. Because you may be paid to participate, and college students are almost always looking for money, it's a natural fit. There are ads on television, solicitations online, and requests for participation in newspapers from coast to coast. How can you find out what studies are being conducted and how you can participate? Because there isn't a single Web site dedicated to research trials, search for research studies in your community. In addition to studies, there are many clinical trials discussed in Chapter 6, "Personal Wills: Drugs, Diets, and Devices."

Although this information can be of great service to researchers, it can also be used for other purposes, such as to market certain products to you. Be sure your information is going to a trusted recipient who won't sell your information (unless you give him or her permission to sell it). With that said, it would be unfair not to tell you that a great deal of your information, including health information, is collected regularly by merchants. Every time you buy a bottle of cough syrup and use your frequent shopper's card, the grocery store has a record of your purchase. The same is true for your health insurance billing information. Your insurer keeps a record of what medications are paid for by your insurance, as well as the tests you take. Although

HIPAA requires that your personal health information remain private, aspects of it aren't, including information recorded on some online medical registration Web sites that you, not your provider, complete. In addition, if you're diagnosed with an infectious disease, the state where you live may require that it be reported to the state health board. There's not much you can do about this, but because it's *your* information, you should know about these practices.

One of the positive ways that your personal health information may be used is for the study of quality further facilitated by the Patient Safety and Quality Improvement Act of 2005. This act established patient safety organizations, or PSOs, that keep track of mistakes and subpar treatment of patients. This information has, in the past, been underreported. With this act, that may change. This information may help us find solutions to quality problems in the future. As it's currently envisioned, information will be delivered to a PSO, without the threat of liability or other action as a result of mistakes, thus allowing a free flow of information to problem solve. The PSO should be able to assist the reporting entity with finding solutions to the problems. The focus is on the delivery of care and the improvement of quality. This is an exciting time for both patients and providers.

No matter how you decide to donate, your donations are not only appreciated, but they're also incredibly useful. So, again, thank you.

Selfless Contribution Wants

- Learn about patient advocacy groups that can help you learn more about your disease or condition.
- If you're interested, sign up to be a blood donor, bone marrow donor, or organ donor.
- Consider participation in trials and studies.

11

Selfless Contribution Wishes: Individual Purpose, Production, and Protection

A volunteer is someone who offers service of his or her own free will. According to the United States Bureau of Labor Statistics, about 65.4 million people volunteered from September 2004 through September 2005, averaging 50 hours of time spent pitching in. The key to making your volunteering purposeful and productive is to find the experience that works best for you and to make the most of it.

A Guide to Goal Setting

We're all different, with different interests, skills, talents, and preferences. Some of you may enjoy coaching local sports teams. Others stock shelves at a food pantry. Leadership roles attract some folks.

The trick is evaluating what makes you tick, finding the best opportunity, and making it work for you.

In deciding what you want to do, AARP (www.aarp.org) suggests that you ask yourself the following questions:

- Why am I interested in volunteering?
- What type of activities am I interested in?
- What are my natural strengths and gifts? What do I really enjoy doing?
- Would I prefer a small local organization or a larger regional or national one?
- What issues do I care most about?
- How will my desire to serve fit in with my current time commitments?
- How much time do I want to give? What days or parts of days?
- Would I prefer to do something in my own neighborhood or travel to another?

Be true to yourself when you answer these questions. They'll help you decide what type of organization you want to help, how much you can help, and how you can help.

An Added Bonus

In 2006, if you drive for charity, you can deduct 14 cents on your individual tax return for each charitable mile driven (if you itemize your deductions). Alternatively, you can deduct the cost of the oil and gas you actually used (although that can be hard to measure). You may also deduct transportation, lodging, and meal expenses when you're donating your time away from home to a qualified charitable organization. Just be sure to keep your receipts and good records!

The RGK Center for Philanthropy and Community Service at the LBJ School of Public Affairs at the University of Texas at Austin (www.ServiceLeader.org) also makes suggestions for evaluating volunteer opportunities:

- When shopping for a volunteer job, arrange to tour the agency, speak with paid staff or unpaid staff (volunteers), and learn about the organization and its volunteer program. Get the organization's brochure, look at its Web site, and educate yourself about what the organization is trying to accomplish.

- Ask the agency why it involves volunteers and how volunteers help the organization work toward its mission. The answer will give you an idea of the value of volunteers to the agency and the kind of culture in which they operate.

- Ask about written volunteer job descriptions and length of commitment, inquire about training opportunities, and discuss your motivation for and interest in volunteering.

- You should expect to be interviewed by agency representatives who are responsible for determining the appropriateness of potential volunteers.

- Remember that you will be expected to complete the assignment you've accepted and perform the job to the best of your ability. Just as you're investing your time in the organization, the staff and other volunteers are investing time and resources in you.

- Be patient—not every volunteer job is right for every volunteer. It is important to give yourself time to explore a variety of opportunities within the different agencies. While one particular job may not be ideal for you, dozens of other volunteer assignments may meet your needs and expectations.

We know firsthand that volunteering can be frustrating, especially if you feel overwhelmed or underappreciated. You also want all of your hard work to benefit others. Don't be afraid to ask the hard questions—you want your volunteer donations to help everyone, including yourself.

Once you find your passion, you'll be on the path to finding the best opportunity for you. If you need some help finding the right organization, log onto one of the following Web sites:

- **www.volunteermatch.org**—A nonprofit organization dedicated to matching up volunteers.

- **www.worldvolunteerweb.org**—A volunteer matching service provided by the United Nations.

- **www.usafreedomcorps.gov/**—A partnership among several U.S. government agencies to provide an easy-to-use source for volunteer opportunities.

And let's not forget, doing good for others is also an opportunity to do good for yourself. You'll find greater purpose. Volunteering will bring balance to your life. The direction that participation can bring may alleviate or stop depression. It's another great reason to join in! At some point, you have been or will be the beneficiary of volunteerism. Return the favor or pay it forward.

A Guide to Time Management

As much as we like to think we can do it all, we'll admit it, we can't. Neither can you. In addition to deciding what cause you're interested in and what's important to you, you need to determine how much time you can contribute. Notice we use the word "cause," not "causes." Part of being a productive volunteer is managing your time, and the best way to do that is to commit to just one organization. When you spend your time running from task to task and charity to charity, you expend more energy on getting from here to there than you do for your favorite group. You can end up multitasking to the point of accomplishing nothing.

One of our favorite phrases is "Stick to your knitting." It means doing what you do best. You'll make the most of your volunteer opportunity if you do just that. When you focus your interests and your talents, you can do more. Are you great with numbers? Offer bookkeeping services. Do you work wonders with a paintbrush? There are many charities dedicated to improving living conditions for the less fortunate. Or perhaps you're a retired marketing executive. Almost any organization would love your ideas on sharing its message with the general public. Use your skills to help the organization you're interested in improving. You have the talent; make the most of it for others.

Within your capacity as a volunteer, make sure you're not duplicating someone else's efforts. Reinventing the wheel is pointless—be different or take a different tack. No one needs too much of a good thing. We'll give you the Warren Buffett example. He could have started his own charity, but instead he gave his money to Bill Gates' foundation. Not only was Mr. Buffett incredibly generous, but he made a thoughtful, effective, and efficient gift. You want your volunteer donations to be the same.

Vivacious Volunteers

How can you be a great volunteer? Follow our suggestions!

- Be reliable. Meet your obligations, be on time, and be dependable.
- Be happy, enthusiastic, and excited to be donating your time.
- Be secretive. Keep confidential info classified.
- Be respectful, courteous, thoughtful, and friendly.
- Be well prepared. Understand your assignment, ask questions if you need to, and do your best to complete your tasks.
- Be an advocate. Share your experiences with friends. Pass along your organization's message. Spread the word!

If the organization doesn't appreciate your talents or time donations, find one that does. You want to feel great about your hard work,
not discouraged or annoyed. That's why it's critical to surround yourself with individuals who understand what you have to offer. Beware
of power struggles—if you don't mesh with the staff and other volunteers, move on. Not only do you need to match your talents, but you
also need to match your comfort level.

A Guide to Liability Protection

If you're involved in any type of leadership position, you need to protect yourself. The same is true for leadership in a charitable organization. Before you volunteer, be sure the organization is adequately
insured. If you're joining the leadership ranks, be sure your organization of choice has officer and director insurance. Inquire as to any
possible liability for your participation. Learn the rules of the game.

Should your volunteer service lead you to the boardroom, we
strongly encourage you to bring your inner inquisitor. Ask the right
questions—of everything. In recent reviews of nonprofit organizations by both the U.S. Senate Finance Committee and the Internal
Revenue Service, charities with boards that weren't active in the
management and oversight of the organization's operations often ran
afoul of regulations. When you accept a board position, you accept
great responsibility. If you're not comfortable with this position of
authority, defer to a position within the organization with less
accountability.

Being aware is especially important if your charity of choice deals
with health care and protected health information (PHI). PHI is governed by many government regulations, violations of which may
result in significant fines and other penalties. Again, ask the right
questions, especially if you're in a position of responsibility.

If you're a donor in the true sense of the word, there's no liability to you for contributions of blood, tissue, and organs. However, if you're aware (or even think) that you may have infectious diseases or any other conditions that may make your contribution unusable, share this information.

Again, we applaud you for supporting charitable organizations and the medical and scientific communities!

Selfless Contribution Wishes

- Decide what you want to do—your goals.
- Research volunteer opportunities.
- Confirm that you have liability protection when you pitch in to help.
- Be a great volunteer!

12

Selfless Contribution Wills: Donation Requirements, Responsibilities, and Rights

Your generosity in donating of yourself requires responsibility and accountability on the part of the entity receiving your donation. In this chapter, we'll talk about donation requirements and responsibilities, as well as your rights as a donor.

A Guide to Informed Consent

Whenever you volunteer to be a participant in a clinical trial or study or, for that matter, undergo any medical procedure or treatment, you must give your *informed* consent. Informed consent requires you to be told all aspects of a clinical trial or medical intervention, including what will happen, what could happen, and everything else, good and bad. You have to understand, and communicate your understanding, before you can become a subject. That's why it's called informed consent. You're giving your authorization to participate in writing. This consent is specific. If the study, trial, procedure, or treatment changes, a new consent is required.

Three specific situations require your informed consent: organ donation, tissue for research, and outcome information. Organ donation is strongly encouraged in the United States. That's why you have an option to be an organ donor when you renew your driver's license. Checking the box that says "yes" on the back of your license is the simplest form of informed consent.

Can I Revoke My Informed Consent?

Absolutely. You can revoke your informed consent at any time. Tell your doctor, research coordinator, or study coordinator that you no longer wish to participate and want to revoke your consent.

Because national and local laws are constantly changing, so are consent forms. In addition to details about the procedure or trial, its side effects, and pros and cons, consent forms must disclose that the information you provide could unintentionally be revealed. Not only will you be given the opportunity to read the disclosures, but you should also be given a chance to discuss them with a representative of the research team or someone from your physician's office. This is the time to ask questions. And, as we say to our clients and patients, there are no dumb questions.

Informed consent is regulated by an institutional review board (IRB). IRBs are independent ethics committees that, within rules set by the FDA and the Department of Health and Human Services, review research proposals and approve, disprove, or request changes for a proposed study or trial. IRBs, found at both the local and national level, act as oversight boards to make sure research conducted on humans is ethical, scientific, and meets all relevant regulations. Medical experts, community leaders, and trained laypeople serve on IRBs.

How does it work? We'll give you an example. Researcher X, who works at pharmaceutical company Y, discovers a compound that is now ready to be tested on humans. Before getting IRB approval, pharmaceutical company Y finds a treating physician to become the trial's principal investigator. It's the principal investigator who devises and runs the trial. Once the trial specifics are determined, IRB approval is requested. If there's no IRB approval, there's no trial or study.

A Guide to Record Keeping and Reporting

Record keeping and reporting comes in many shapes and sizes. We'll start with your decision to be an organ donor. Make sure your decision is reflected on your driver's license. It should also be included in your Living Will and Health Care Proxy. Explain to your health care representative that this is what you want. The same is true if you're interested in donating your body to science. Leave explicit instructions for your loved ones. When you're a blood and tissue donor, there are no reporting requirements. Still, it's a good idea to fill in your physician on everything you do related to your health.

Scientific Data

If you're a study participant, the terms of the study will outline your reporting requirements. This can be an ongoing and complicated process. Some studies go on for life, such as the Framingham Heart Study or the Nurses' Health Study.

How is your data collected? You'll likely be required to show up on set dates and times. The researchers will probably ask you lots of questions, maybe take blood or other fluid samples, and, depending on the study, ask you to take diagnostic tests like a CT or bone scan, for example. If you have side effects, you'll be asked to rank their severity on a scale of 0 to 4.

What are the researchers going to do with all this info? After they collect the data, they'll pool it with others to see if there are any trends. They group side effects into two categories: adverse events and serious adverse events. An adverse event (AE) is anything that goes wrong that isn't life threatening or that requires a change in the treatment protocol. A serious adverse event (SAE) is life threatening. The SAEs are passed through the system in a rapid manner. If the SAEs reach statistical significance, it could result in the study or trial being shut down.

The researchers then analyze the collected data and send it to a review committee. The review committee is independent of the research group, with no financial interest in the research results. This independent evaluation is needed before sending data regarding a device or drug to the FDA. Once the research is final, the data is compiled and a research paper written. If the results are considered relevant, a peer review is done to ensure that the study was completed appropriately. The next step is journal publication. The final step is a decision whether to move to the next trial phase or study level.

A Guide to Donation Ownership

It may seem that once you've made a donation, what you've donated is no longer yours. But that's not necessarily the case with regard to tissue donations. For example, if you give a sample of your DNA for the sole purpose of studying breast cancer, the same sample can't be used to research the genetic tendency toward high blood pressure.

The only way this change can be made is to ask you to sign a new informed consent form.

Donations of DNA aren't limited to situations requiring your informed consent. You've probably read about discovering who your ancestors are through DNA. Certain companies, using your DNA sample, can tell you that you're related to the famous (or perhaps the infamous). Well, as much as you want to uncover your family legacy, when you give your DNA away without giving your informed consent, you've turned over your entire personal information database (also known as your **genome**) to an unregulated entity. Because there's no IRB governing these companies and how they use your data, who knows what could happen.

Modern medicine wouldn't be where it is today without your participation. Organ and tissue donations save lives. Trial and study participants find cures. Volunteers improve situations for others. While each donor and volunteer may be a small cog in the wheel of progress, together you're driving the health care system forward. Give yourself a big pat on the back for the role you're playing, no matter how big or small.

Selfless Contribution Wills

- Be sure you've given your informed consent.
- Keep good records.
- Learn who owns your donation.

Section V

The Wants, Wishes, and Wills of Your Estate Planning

At this point in the book, we could offer you lots of proverbs that inspire you to act (you know, "Better late than never," "Never put off till tomorrow what may be done today," and "One of these days is none of these days"). And although we're tempted to pull out all the stops in encouraging you to plan, plan, plan, we recognize that you're reading this book, so you already realize that you should be doing *something*.

That's where Section V comes in. The next three chapters outline issues for you to consider and the *somethings* you can do today to ensure that your wants, wishes, and wills are fulfilled on your passing.

There may be a part of you that's thinking, "Why is all this necessary? My loved ones know what I want. Isn't that enough?" Sadly, it's not. There are laws and miscommunications that may keep your wishes from being carried out. You need to be specific, thoughtful, and organized. And that's what we're here to help you do.

13

Estate Planning Wants: Purpose, Preparation, and Protection

Estate planning. It sounds intimidating, as if it's only meant for the Park Avenue, mega-wealthy types, right? The fact is, nothing could be further from the truth. Estate planning is for everyone, whether you have $5,000 or $5,000,000 to your name.

What exactly *is* estate planning? It's, quite simply, a strategic plan to distribute your assets, including your home, car, investments, and special effects, such as your wedding ring or family photos, upon your death. It allows *you* to choose *who* will receive your savings and treasured items. And once you've decided the *who*, estate planning lets you decide *how* your assets are distributed. Your plan can be complex or simple. You can use a will, a trust, or a combination of the two. Or maybe you'll use beneficiary designations to ensure that your assets go to certain individuals. There are countless options, which we'll explain in this section. As you keep reading, remember that estate planning is about *your* wants, wishes, and wills.

Before discussing why estate planning is important, we want to briefly explain what happens to your assets after you die. This process is referred to as **estate administration**. Although it may seem that we're putting the cart before the horse, it's helpful to understand estate administration before deciding how best to plan your estate.

Except in some exceedingly rare situations, every person who dies has assets. How these assets are owned, or titled, at death determines what happens next.

Beneficiary Designations

Certain investments, such as life insurance, retirement plans, annuities, payable on death (POD) accounts, and individual retirement arrangements, allow you to select a beneficiary. The **beneficiary** is the person or people you want to receive the asset when you die. You name them on a beneficiary designation form supplied by the insurance company, your employer, your bank, or the investment firm managing the asset. If there is a properly completed beneficiary designation, it doesn't matter what your will says since the proceeds will be inherited by your named beneficiary or beneficiaries, even if your will says something different. What happens if there is no beneficiary named or your beneficiary has died? The beneficiary then becomes your estate and your will, if you have one, determines who receives the assets.

Double Check Those Designations

As part of your estate plan, review your beneficiary designations. Make sure you've named the person or people you want to receive these assets. Contact your life insurance agent, your financial planner, the bank, the veteran's administration, or your employer's human resources department if you can't find copies of the designations. Ask your attorney to review them to make sure you've completed them correctly and they don't jeopardize your estate plan. If you've been divorced, it's extremely important to review the designations. A former spouse is prohibited by law from receiving anything under a will written when you were still married. However, if he or she is the named beneficiary of a life insurance policy or retirement account, for example, his or her bank account will get a lot bigger when you die because a beneficiary designation usually isn't affected by a divorce decree. Trust us, we've found that many individuals can't remember who they named and are shocked to realize that, despite being divorced decades ago, their ex is the named beneficiary of an old life insurance policy.

Joint Tenants

The most common forms of joint tenancy assets are bank and brokerage accounts and real estate. The best example is a joint checking account. Check the title on a bank account. If you see the letters JTWROS (Joint Tenants with Rights of Survivorship) or JT TEN (Joint Tenants), it's a **joint tenancy account**. There can be more than two joint tenants. Assets owned as joint tenants with the right of survivorship will pass to your joint tenant on your death, no matter what your will might say. Another form of joint tenancy is **tenancy by the entirety**, which can only be between a husband and a wife. Today, we usually see this only with real estate.

Tenants-in-Common

Joint tenancy and tenancy by the entirety are different from tenants-in-common. Each tenant in a **tenancy-in-common** ownership owns an undivided interest in the property or asset. But on the death of a tenant, his or her share becomes part of his or her estate. It does not pass to the other tenants. Any asset that can be owned as a joint tenant can also be owned as a tenant-in-common. If you're unsure how property or an account is titled, check with your financial planner, lawyer, or the branch manager of the bank where you have your account.

Individual Assets

Individual assets are those without a beneficiary designation and in your name alone. They could be a car, checking account, shares of stock, or real estate. If you're the only one that owns it, it's an individual asset.

Individual assets, together with any part of a tenants-in-common asset, form your **estate**. How these assets are distributed, as we noted earlier, is part of your estate plan.

Get Organized!

One of the best things you can do to simplify the administration of your estate is to get organized. Nothing is more difficult during the administration process than finding assets here and there. For example, a person might have five bank accounts with $55 at five locations, two shares of stock in 15 different companies still in certificate form, or old savings bonds that matured when disco was still the rage. Get rid of all the old stock certificates by opening a brokerage account and transferring all of your shares of stock into a single account. You don't need certificates of deposit at five banks. Keep all of your accounts at one institution (the FDIC insures deposits up to $100,000 at one institution). Leave a detailed Letter of Instruction. (See Chapter 16, "Legacy Wants: Providing Ideas, Intentions, and Instructions.") Not only will your loved ones benefit, but so will the new, organized you.

In Chapter 15, "Estate Planning Wills: Testaments, Trusts, and Other Tools," we discuss how to implement your estate plan by using wills and trusts. But what happens to your will and trusts when you die? It depends on your estate plan and the state in which you reside.

You've probably heard the term probate. **Probate** is the court "proceeding" that proves a Last Will and Testament to be valid or invalid. If your will is valid, your named executor or personal representative is provided with Letters Testamentary authorizing him or her to act on behalf of your estate. If there is no valid will and you die **intestate** (described in the following section, "A Guide to the Purposes and Benefits of Estate Planning"), one of your relatives may apply to the appropriate court for Letters of Administration, which would allow him or her to act on behalf of your intestate estate. Each state is different, but generally a spouse or child would be the first individual considered to fulfill the role of administrator. The appointed administrator may be required to obtain a surety bond in the approximate amount of the estate assets. A **surety bond** is like an insurance policy to ensure that the administrator does his or her job.

Who Are These People?

Administrator—The individual or financial institution appointed to oversee the estate of a person dying without a valid will or if there is no named executor or personal representative. Also referred to as an **administratrix**.

Executor—The individual or financial institution that carries out the provisions of a will. Also referred to as an **executrix** or **personal representative**.

Fiduciary—An individual or financial institution acting for the benefit of an estate, trust, or person. Includes **executor**, **trustee**, **guardian**, and **administrator**.

Testator—The individual leaving a valid will at his or her death. Also referred to as a **testatrix**.

Trustee—The individual or financial institution that administers a trust.

You may have heard a lot about the need to "avoid probate" at all costs. Probate in certain states can be very expensive, with probate costs tied to the value of the estate. For example, in Florida, California, New York, and Massachusetts, the probate process is cumbersome, time consuming, and requires a great deal of court involvement. Alternatively, in some states, such as Pennsylvania and New Jersey, the probate process is incredibly simple and inexpensive with little involvement by the courts. Where you live, therefore, may influence how your estate plan is implemented. We'll talk more about this in Chapter 15.

A Guide to the Purposes and Benefits of Estate Planning

Let's face it, most of us want our hard-earned money to go where we want it to go, whether it's to our loved ones or a favorite charity. And we want it to be used for the purposes we intend, especially if the beneficiary is a child or a disabled person. But if we don't specify these things, they will be decided by the laws of the state in which we reside. Says Joanne, age 32:

> *Much of my family has a plan in place in case of death, and everyone is happier as a result.*

The state will decide if you don't? That's right. If you die without a will or other testamentary document (for instance, a trust), you have died intestate—without "testifying to your wishes"—and the intestacy laws of the state where you live determine who will receive your assets.

In Kentucky, for example, if you die intestate and own real estate, your real estate will first pass to your children or the descendants (your grandchildren or great-grandchildren) of any child of yours who has already died. If you have no children, it passes to your father and mother, or the survivor of them. If neither of your parents is living, it goes to your brothers and sisters or their descendants if they're not then living. And if you don't have siblings, your real estate goes to your spouse. If your spouse isn't living or you're not married, it's left to your grandparents or their descendants (which means your aunts and uncles or your cousins). So let's think about this. If you're married and you own real estate in your name only, and you don't have a will, your spouse will only receive your property if you aren't survived by your children, your parents, your siblings, or your nieces and nephews. This may be what you want—but we bet a lot of you would rather have your spouse receive your real estate before some of your nieces and nephews.

Let's consider Florida. If you die without a will, and you're married and don't have descendants (children, grandchildren, or great-grandchildren), your spouse gets everything. If you're married with descendants and the descendants are also your spouse's descendants, your spouse receives the first $60,000, plus half of your remaining estate; your descendants receive the other half. If your descendants are *not* your spouse's descendants, your surviving spouse receives half and your descendants the other half. If you're not married, your assets pass to your descendants, and if none, to your parents. If your parents aren't living, your estate goes to your siblings or their descendants, and if none, to your grandparents or their children (your aunts and uncles), then to your cousins, and then to the "kin of your last deceased spouse." Finally, if you have no living relatives, your estate passes to the state of Florida to be used for the state's school fund.

And then there's New Jersey. The intestacy laws are similar to Florida, with two exceptions. First, if you're a registered domestic partner in New Jersey (New Jersey allows homosexual couples and unmarried couples over the age of 62 to register as domestic partners), your domestic partner is treated as a spouse. Second, if you're survived by a spouse and no descendants, your spouse receives the first 25% of your estate (but not less than $50,000 or more than

$200,000) plus three-quarters of the balance of your estate, with your parents getting the rest of your estate. If your parents aren't living, your spouse gets it all. Third, if you don't have living relatives, then your stepchildren or their descendants will receive your estate. What's important is that these stepchildren don't have to be your last spouse's kids. That means the children of your first spouse whom you haven't spoken to in 30 years could benefit from your estate. Yikes!

What About In-Laws and Adopted Children?

Legally adopted children are treated as natural children in most circumstances. If you don't want an adopted child to take a share of your estate, your will must specifically state this. Unless you name an in-law in your will, your in-laws (or out-laws as we've heard them described!) will not be beneficiaries of your estate.

Again, would the preceding distribution of your assets reflect what you want? We doubt it. If you're cohabiting, for example, your significant other would get nothing but heartache when you die. And if you're gay, unless you live in one of a handful of states, your partner would be out of luck. So what do you do? Make sure you have a valid will or other testamentary document. Of the hundreds of individuals we surveyed for this book, most said that caring for their loved ones on their death was their biggest concern. So why let the government determine who receives your assets when *you* can decide?

Harold Ivan Smith, in his book *Finding Your Way to Say Good-bye*, agrees:

> *Not having a will sabotages and complicates your loved one's grief. They will, of necessity, spend time and money in an attorney's office as they survive the legal and financial maze. They will expend incredible emotional, and perhaps financial, capital trying to settle your estate.*

Exactly. Sally, age 37, adds,

The benefits of estate planning are immeasurable to other family members.

That's yet another reason why you should make estate planning a priority.

What Does Escheat Mean?

We're often asked, "Is it true that, if I die without a will, everything I have will go to the state?" The answer: It depends. In many states, if you die intestate and you have absolutely no living relative, your assets pass, or **escheat**, to the state in which you live. So, it can happen, but only if you have absolutely no living relative when you die and you have no will directing that your assets go to friends or charitable organizations.

In addition to deciding who benefits from your estate, you can pick who acts on behalf of your estate. This is your executor or personal representative. It's a job that usually lasts for a year or two, depending on the size and complexity of your estate. Your will could also name a trustee to control funds for your beneficiaries.

Perhaps the most important reason of all to have an estate plan, and specifically a will, is to name a guardian for your minor or disabled children. It's critical that you identify and name the person you want to raise your children if you die. We discuss these positions at length in Chapter 15.

Of course, the amount of planning that is required will depend, for example, on the value of your assets, your wants and wishes, taxes (if any), and the age and health of your beneficiaries.

A Guide to Protecting Your Estate from Taxes

As Margaret Mitchell wrote in *Gone with the Wind*, "Death and taxes and childbirth! There's never any convenient time for any of them." Make them death taxes, and you've just put two of life's inconveniences together. That's right: Depending on where you live, the size of your estate, and who your heirs are, there may be taxes due upon your demise.

There are several different death taxes. Let's start with state taxes. Depending on your state of residence, there may be an inheritance tax or state estate tax. Generally, an inheritance tax is determined by who receives assets from your estate and what their relationship is to you. In New Jersey, for example, there is no inheritance tax if the beneficiary of your estate is a spouse, child, grandchild, parent, or charity. If you leave your estate to a friend or cousin, the tax is about 15 percent. The tax on property received by brothers and sisters and children-in-law is 11 percent. In Kentucky, there is no inheritance tax due if your beneficiary is a parent, child, grandchild, sibling, or spouse. Kentucky's inheritance tax ranges from 4 to 16 percent for beneficiaries who are children-in-law, aunts, uncles, nieces, nephews, and great-grandchildren. If you're anyone else, including a cousin, the inheritance tax falls between 6 and 16 percent. Of course, imposition of inheritance taxes is a little more complicated than this, but we wanted to provide you with some examples.

In addition to an inheritance tax, there may also be a state estate tax. Before 2001, state estate taxes were directly linked to the federal estate tax and the state death tax credit. That's no longer the case, which has drastically decreased the taxes paid to the states. Some states have responded by creating their own tax structure. New Jersey "decoupled" from the federal estate tax structure, which means if you have a taxable estate greater than $675,000, New Jersey estate tax will likely be imposed. Florida doesn't have taxes on death, or any income tax for that matter. (It's not just the warm weather than makes everyone retire to the Sunshine State!) Talk to your accountant and attorney to learn more about the current tax laws in your state.

So now we get to federal taxes. There's been a lot of discussion about the federal estate tax. Currently, an estate valued at over $2,000,000 must file a federal estate tax return. The maximum tax rate is 45 percent. Here's an example: If you die in 2007 and have a taxable estate of $2,500,000 (all of your assets less any deductions, such as funeral expenses, attorney fees, medical bills, and money left to an American spouse), the federal estate tax due would be approximately $230,000. Not exactly a small number, would you agree?

The Changing Federal Tax Law

In 2007 and 2008, if your estate exceeds $2,000,000, your estate is required to file a federal estate tax return. This filing threshold increases to $3,500,000 in 2009. Under current law, there is no estate tax in 2010, with the filing requirement dropping back to $1,000,000 in 2011 and thereafter. With that said, there are several bills before Congress to reduce the federal estate tax. While we can't guess what our legislators will decide, folks in the know believe that there will be some change in the federal estate tax laws. State tax structures will likely change in response to any federal change. If your estate exceeds $2,000,000, talk to a lawyer to be sure your estate plan factors in any future tax law changes.

There's one other federal tax you may have heard about. It's called the federal generation skipping transfer tax. If you decide to leave assets to someone who is two generations younger than you, an additional tax is imposed. The objective is to discourage folks from skipping their children and leaving assets directly to their grandchildren. This tax doesn't apply to small inheritances. In 2007, it applies only to transfers over $2,000,000.

So now you understand the other piece of the estate planning puzzle: tax reduction. Betsy's aunt failed to complete her planning. The result, as Betsy, age 52, puts it:

Uncle Sam is sucking the life out of the estate.

If deciding who you want to receive your estate isn't enough incentive, estate planning can often reduce taxes due on your passing.

You're probably thinking, "There's no way I have enough money to worry about this!" Well, get out your calculator and let's see. To determine if you might have a taxable estate for federal or state purposes, start adding up your assets. Consider the value today of the following:

- All real estate, including your home. If you own the home jointly with another, only include the value of your share.
- All retirement accounts, profit sharing plans, individual retirement arrangements, and 401(k) plans.
- Bank accounts.
- Stocks, bonds, and brokerage accounts.
- Business or partnership interests.
- Life insurance. If you own and control a life insurance policy, the face value of the policy proceeds is included in your estate for estate tax purposes. This includes any insurance you have through your employer as well as any policy purchased independently.
- Trust accounts. If you're the beneficiary of a trust, it might be considered an asset of your estate for tax purposes if you have the power to decide who receives the trust assets at your death. This is called a **power of appointment**.
- Value of any taxable gifts you made during your lifetime.

- Everything else that you own, including cars, boats, RVs, paintings, jewelry—you name it. If you own it, it's an asset of your estate and is included for estate tax purposes. If you don't know what the value is, ask an appraiser or check the Internet.

Don't be tempted to exclude certain items from your estate just because you think the IRS won't find out. We've sat through many audits. The IRS knows what to look for, and they'll find it. Honesty is always the best policy. Robin, age 58, recounts her experience:

My aunt and father were secretive about their financial holdings.... During the estate administration process, we filed 14 tax returns between the two of them and paid out six figures in estate taxes that could have been much further reduced had they been proactive rather than secretive.

If the dollar value of your assets exceeds $2,000,000 and you die in the year 2007 or 2008, your estate will be required to file a federal estate tax return. If you're like many people, you had no idea that you had such a big estate.

Now, whether tax will be due is dependent on your deductions. You receive a deduction for all items left to your spouse if your spouse is a U.S. citizen, as well as charitable bequests made at death. All of the expenses associated with your death, such as debts, medical bills, funeral expenses, and attorney and accountant fees, are deductions. Subtract this figure from the value of your assets. If you still exceed $2,000,000 and die in 2007 or 2008, federal tax may be due from your estate. Whether or not you'll be required to file a state estate tax return depends on the laws of your state. The same holds true for an inheritance tax return. That's another good reason to consult an attorney or tax advisor.

Unfortunately, there's one more tax to add to the mix—income tax. Generally, an inheritance is not income to a beneficiary. He or she doesn't report inherited assets on his or her Form 1040. The exception is receipt of an IRA (traditional or Roth) or other retirement benefit (such as a 401(k) or profit sharing plan). Unless a retirement account or IRA is rolled over or continued for the lifetime of a beneficiary, any lump sum payout is income to the beneficiary. In other words, if Father Joe leaves his $50,000 IRA to his son Scott, and Scott takes a lump sum distribution, Scott has to pay income tax on this $50,000. Advise your loved ones to talk to their accountants and attorneys before deciding what to do with this type of asset to avoid any unanticipated income tax problems. Read Ed Slott's *Parlay Your IRA into a Family Fortune* for some terrific advice on making the most of your retirement assets.

After you die, your executor or personal representative must file your final income tax return. If you die on September 26, for example, an income tax return must be filed on your behalf for all income earned from January 1 through September 26. After that, any income earned by your estate must be reported as income. This requires the filing of a fiduciary income tax return (Form 1041). An estate may use a calendar year or a fiscal year for income tax filing purposes. Because any additional talk about income taxes will put you to sleep, we recommend talking to your tax preparer for more information.

Is there anything you can do to reduce taxes on your death? You bet. There are many options, from establishing trusts, to making gifts during your lifetime, to giving to charities, either during life or at death. See Chapters 14 ("Estate Planning Wishes: Caring for Family, Friends, and Foundations") and 15 for more information.

A Guide to Finding Estate Planning Professionals

Now that you know a thing or two about estate planning and taxes, the next step is to find a knowledgeable attorney to guide you in the estate planning process and to assist you in the preparation of the necessary legal documents. Although we've provided you a great deal of important information, it's best to use a qualified professional to prepare documents tailored to your individual circumstances, assets, and wishes.

Our best suggestion for finding the appropriate person is to ask for a referral from a friend, financial planner, colleague, or other advisor. The word-of-mouth reference from someone who has worked with a particular attorney is invaluable. If this isn't helpful, we suggest you contact the lawyer referral service of your local or state bar association, which can give you a list of attorneys specializing in estate planning. If you're worried about cost, check with your local Legal Aid office to see if it can assist you. Another alternative is searching one or more of the following Web sites:

- **American College of Trust and Estate Counsel (www. actec.org)**—ACTEC fellows are attorneys experienced in the preparation of wills and trusts and all areas of estate planning.

- **National Academy of Elder Law Attorneys (www.naela. com)**—NAELA members focus on the needs of elderly and disabled individuals.

- **American Bar Association Lawyer Locator (www.abanet. org)**—This database allows you to search by specialty, including trusts and estates.

- **Martindale-Hubbell Lawyer Locator (www.martindale. com)**—This database allows you to search by specialty, including trusts and estates.

Once you've identified a prospective attorney, be sure to ask up front about the hourly fees, the attorney's expertise and experience, and an approximate time frame for him or her to prepare the necessary documents. Don't be afraid to ask questions. If you don't like the responses or don't receive a response, move to the next name on your list.

Time Waits for No One

Tell your lawyer—whether he or she's a high-priced counselor or a free attorney at the legal aid office—your time frame for putting your estate plan into place, especially if you're sick or taking a long trip in the near future. Ask when you can expect to see draft documents. If you don't receive them when promised, call, e-mail, or write. The fact is, the squeaky client often receives his or her documents first. And if your attorney can't meet your timeline, find one who can. No one should have to wait months for a response from his or her counselor!

Before meeting with your attorney, think twice about whom, if anyone, you want to bring. If you're married and have children from a previous marriage, for example, you may wish to meet with an attorney without your spouse. Likewise, if your children argue constantly or you intend to treat them differently in your estate planning documents, you're better off going without them. Also, don't use an attorney recommended by or already representing these family members. Any perceived conflict of interest could cause problems with your will after you pass away—something everyone wants to avoid.

Yes, lawyers can be expensive, so you may be tempted to create your own estate plan using books or forms that you find on the Internet. We can't emphasize enough the importance of individualized attention and discussion with a member of the bar specializing in estate planning. An "unofficial" will or a will that isn't signed with the required formalities can cause even more problems than no will. Christopher Luongo, Esq., Deputy Surrogate of the Morris County Surrogate's Court, Morristown, New Jersey, agrees:

> We see the biggest problems and the saddest outcomes when people 'do it themselves' because they think they're saving money, and ultimately they don't.

It's also important to avoid "bargain basement" estate plans. If an attorney offers you a will for $250, chances are you're dealing with someone who isn't well versed in estate planning or who's simply giving you a form will. It may cost a little more for a tailored estate plan, but it's money well spent.

The best way to reduce attorney fees is to come to your meeting prepared. The more detailed information you're able to provide at your initial meeting, the less time your lawyer will have to spend calling to ask additional questions, getting the spelling of names, and so on. So in addition to your full legal name (and any other names you use), address, and social security number, be sure to bring the following:

- Legal names and addresses of your spouse, domestic partner, children, grandchildren, siblings, parents, and friends you would like to benefit under your will. Make a notation if any individual is disabled as well as the ages of each individual. Let your lawyer know if any beneficiary is *not* a U.S. citizen.

- A current list of what your assets are, how much they're valued, and how they're owned (joint tenancy, sole ownership, and so on). Remember to include life insurance policies, real estate, personal property, automobiles, business interests, retirement benefits, individual retirement arrangements, brokerage accounts, stock certificates, and so on. If you're unsure whether to include it on the list, include it anyway.

- A current list of your liabilities, such as mortgages and other debts.

- Whether you are the beneficiary of any trusts (perhaps created by a parent or grandparent). Bring along a copy of any trust if you have it.

- If you've been divorced, bring a copy of all divorce decrees and settlement agreements. This will assist your attorney in determining whether you have any obligations under the agreements that must be included in your estate planning documents.

- Any prenuptial or antenuptial agreements.

- If you made any big gifts during your lifetime, write down the details. Did you give your daughter $100,000 to buy her first house? Have you made any loans? Bring a list with you.

- A list of any charitable or specific bequests (for example, $10,000 to a local church or favorite niece). Include names and addresses of the beneficiaries.

- A summary of your estate planning goals. For example, providing for your spouse or children, establishing a scholarship fund at your alma mater, paying for your grandchildren's educations, minimizing taxes, or establishing trusts to give incentives to your children. By giving your attorney an idea of your goals, he or she will be able to discuss the right options for you.

- Names of individuals to serve as fiduciaries (executors or personal representatives, trustees, and guardians).

- Information for the preparation of a Power of Attorney, Health Care Proxy, and Living Will. (See Chapter 9, "Medical-Legal Wills: Directives, Definitions, and Discussions.")

- Anything else that's important to you.

Last but not least, be candid with your counselor. Tell him or her *everything*. Hiding information or not being forthcoming will only jeopardize a carefully crafted plan. Don't be embarrassed. You won't be the first to share with your attorney that your son has a gambling problem, you had an out-of-wedlock child in high school, or you're concerned that your daughter will invest her inheritance in her husband's latest business scheme. Problems can't be solved unless they're identified.

Don't Wait Till the Last Minute!

Making your estate planning decisions is hard enough. Don't wait until you're headed out the door on a big vacation or have surgery scheduled to put your affairs in order. There is nothing more stressful than having to run to your attorney's office three hours before your plane leaves or asking your lawyer to visit you in the hospital for a document signing. We all have enough stress, so why add to it?

We hope that we've provided you the information you need to understand the purpose of estate planning and the importance of protecting your assets, both from taxes and the laws of intestacy, and the urgency of preparing the necessary estate planning documents. You have the ability to create the best estate plan for you and your loved ones. Read on for more information on how to do just that.

Estate Planning Wants

- Get organized—make a list of your assets and how they're titled.
- Check and update all beneficiary designations.
- Understand estate and inheritance taxes—and how to minimize them.
- Find an attorney with expertise in estate planning to draft your estate planning documents.

14

Estate Planning Wishes: Caring for Family, Friends, and Foundations

When we started writing this book, we thought of charity as only doing good for those in need. However, the definition of charity—"benevolent goodwill toward or love of humanity"—is much broader. That's why, in this chapter, we focus on the things you can do to care for your family, friends, and nonprofit organizations.

With that said, we want to remind you that the decision to care for others is a personal decision. It isn't for everyone. For some, the goal is to die "when the last check bounces" or to "spend it all" before taking that final breath. If that's the case, we wish you great success. Our experience, though, is that most individuals are concerned about sharing their good fortune with others, whether it's done now or in the future.

A Guide to Planning for Relatives

For many, "charity begins at home." Luckily, there are many ways to take care of your family—starting with the wills and trusts that we discuss in Chapter 15, "Estate Planning Wills: Testaments, Trusts, and Other Tools." But estate planning isn't limited to wills and trusts. It is the overall plan you set in place to distribute your assets in a manner that achieves your goals, including your wish to care for your relatives. What follows are additional things you can consider to share your goodwill with those you love.

Your Parents

Many younger individuals want to provide for their parents. (Elvis Presley did by providing a trust for his daughter, father, and grandmother.) Before you do, though, talk to your parents. If they have sufficient assets, we recommend not leaving your estate to Mom and Dad because it could result in some double taxation: Assets that could be taxed on your death pass to your parents to be taxed on their deaths. In this situation, you can avoid the potential double tax by just leaving these assets to your siblings, for example. But what if your parents need some financial assistance? Again, talk to them. If they're working toward qualifying for Medicaid or other government benefits, any money you leave them could jeopardize their receipt of these benefits. If that's the case, talk to an elder law attorney and provide for them with a supplemental benefits, or special needs, trust. Alternatively, a trust providing your folks with an income stream and principal as needed works well. If drafted correctly, such a fund would not be included in their estates for tax purposes, and you can decide where the money goes when Mom and Dad are no longer living.

How Do I Talk to My Parents About Estate Planning?

When we asked our friends whether they had discussed estate planning with their moms and dads, most said "No." Why? Most didn't want to give their parents the idea that they were trying to find out what their inheritance might be. So what can you do? Bring the subject up in terms of your own planning to get the conversation started. For example, tell your folks you're writing a will. You're planning on providing for your kids only—do they have any suggestions on the best way to do it? Ask if they need some financial help in the event you die first. Tell them you're meeting with a lawyer, and ask if they have any questions that you can ask on their behalf.

Your Young Children

The single biggest concern of every parent who completed our survey was "How do I make sure my kids are taken care of if I die?" Despite these concerns, though, recent studies show that only 26 percent of parents with minor children have a will. As we noted in Chapter 13, "Estate Planning Wants: Purpose, Preparation, and Protection," if you have little ones, you need a will. Period. There is simply no excuse for not having one.

In addition to a will, what can you do to provide for your offspring? You have many options. Many states offer Section 529 plans. This is a state-authorized education savings plan. Funds contributed to a 529 plan grow tax-free. Federal income tax is never imposed as long as the funds are used to pay college expenses. State income tax isn't imposed until funds are used. If the funds aren't used, there may be penalties on withdrawing the funds. Because the plans are sponsored by the state, though, the investment options are limited. There are also Uniform Transfers to Minors Act (UTMA) or Uniform Gifts to Minors Act (UGMA) accounts. These are accounts opened in the name of a child, grandchild, niece, nephew, or other youngster with a parent or other adult serving as custodian. Taxes are paid annually and could be taxed to the parent depending on the child's income level and age. The investment can be in stock, securities, cash, certificates of deposit, and more. When the beneficiary reaches the age of majority (18 in some states, 21 in others), the account is his or hers to control (or spend). Check with a certified financial advisor for more information.

We tell you about "spending" the UGMA or UTMA account for a reason. Although these accounts are terrific for small amounts, we don't recommend them for large gifts to young ones. Our experience has been that large sums of money in the hands of an 18- or 21-year-old often ends up as a few lavish trips to Las Vegas or a very fast car. Unfortunately, teaching children the importance and value of money has not been a priority for many in this country. It often takes several years in the real world for kids to understand saving, nest eggs, and rainy day funds. That's why we encourage our clients who want to make gifts to their children or other young relatives to consider a trust (see Chapter 15). This allows you to determine what the money is used for and when your kids can receive the funds outright.

Disabled Loved Ones

Regrettably, many individuals need a helping hand. We're talking about people suffering from a disability, whether it's emotional, mental, or physical. Our government provides some really terrific benefits to these individuals, young and old. But the benefits provided only go so far. That's why you may want to provide for the "extras" with a supplemental benefits, or special needs, trust. This type of trust does not jeopardize your loved one's government benefits. Instead, it provides a fund that "supplements" the benefits. For example, the trust assets could be used for vacations or to buy a specially equipped vehicle, computer, music equipment—anything else you can think of. An elder and disability law attorney can provide more guidance.

A Guide to Planning for Nonrelatives

Throughout this book, we've used the expression "loved ones." That's because we recognize that, for many, your friends, not blood relatives, are your caregivers, your companions, and your biggest concerns. For some, especially gay and cohabiting couples, having an estate plan is the only way to ensure that these individuals benefit from your estate.

In Chapter 15, we discuss at length wills and trusts. We give examples of providing for spouses and children. The same plans also apply to nonrelatives. You can make a specific bequest to your roommate. You can establish a trust to pay for the college education of a neighbor's child. You can give your possessions and assets to a boyfriend, business partner, or best friend. If you want someone to have something, say it—*in writing*.

It's important not to assume that others will know your wishes. When our colleague Becky, age 32, lost her live-in boyfriend on September 11, his family came to their apartment and started removing all of the furniture and electronics, as well as his personal effects. Although some of the items belonged to Bob, others they had purchased together. Becky couldn't prove this, and Bob's family didn't believe that he'd want her to have his things. Becky, emotionally drained, decided it wasn't worth it to put up a fight. If only Bob had made it clear that he wanted Becky to keep the furniture. But he didn't.

Although we'd all like to think that our families would do the right thing in the face of tragedy, we could fill up every page of this book with examples otherwise. That's why we constantly counsel our clients and patients to clearly express their wishes.

My Charitable Planning Questionnaire

Ask yourself these questions as you consider your estate plan:
- Who could use my help?
- Do they need my help now or in the future?
- What are their particular needs? Is it education? Medical?
- Do any of my loved ones have special needs?
- What are my favorite charities? What are the needs of these charities?
- How can I blend my personal interests and values with the needs of the charity?

A Guide to Planning for Charities

Sharing our good fortune with others is a lesson that our parents taught us. We've both been blessed with professional success and have tried to "give back" both in terms of time and resources. What we've discovered along the way is that behind every opportunity for giving are a thousand other opportunities. We begin with this sentiment so that, as we discuss the many methods of charitable giving, you'll allow yourself to consider the countless ways to give of yourself.

> *The primal duties shine aloft, like stars;*
> *The charities that soothe, and heal, and bless,*
> *Are scattered at the feet of Man, like flowers.*

> —William Wordsworth, "The Excursion," Book ix.

We mention the many charities you can consider, in part, to excite you. Take a moment to consider your passions—the issues that make your blood boil, the images that bring you to tears, and the changes you'd like to see. Allow your mind to wander, to focus on what's important to you. Our point: You don't have to limit your charitable contributions to the big charities that you hear about all the time. You can also look into organizations that are smaller, closer to your home, or perhaps particularly focused on your passions.

Be creative. Long gone are the general donations to the operating funds of charities. Donors can earmark contributions for specific purposes. For example, if you're interested in music, contribute to the music department of your college. If you're interested in finding a cure for cancer, look for a small, start-up charity that supports research of a particular form of cancer or a new method to research cures. Love art? Consider a small museum where your dollars, no matter how modest, will truly be appreciated.

Let the Donor Beware!

If you're not sure a charity is legitimate, log on to the IRS Web site (www.irs.gov) and follow the links to charities to search for authorized charitable organizations. Don't see a particular charity listed? Don't make a contribution.

Our goal is not to pressure you into supporting charitable organizations. That's not for everyone. But if you have an interest in caring for others, we want you to feel fulfilled. We've all read news stories reporting the incredible generosity of Warren Buffett and Bill Gates. You don't have to be a billionaire to make a difference. Every gift, no matter how small or how large, is meaningful.

So how can you give? Where do we start! You can provide for charities during your life or at death. You can create trusts, as well as foundations. Donations can be in cash, securities, and real estate, as well as cars, paintings, and just about anything else.

Charity Begins with the Heart and Ends with the Bottom Line

In addition to giving you a sense of purpose, charitable giving provides some very nice tax benefits. (Just ask Mr. Buffett and Mr. Gates!) Gifts made during life provide an income tax deduction up to 50 percent of your adjusted gross income. (This amount may be reduced depending on your other deductions and income level—check with your tax preparer.) Charitable donations made at death qualify for an estate tax deduction. There is no limit on the deductibility.

As we tell our clients, patients, and friends, making charitable gifts during life has many benefits. First, you get to see your donation in action. Whether it's a single paving stone in a memorial walkway at your local library or a college scholarship for a deserving young student, it's heartwarming to see your contribution at work. Second, you can be a participant in your charity of choice. Perhaps you can provide suggestions, offer some elbow grease, or act as a director or trustee. Third, you get to attend the fun parties. While it may seem superficial to some, attending these events has benefits. You meet other donors, do a little networking, learn about other giving opportunities, and just enjoy some well-deserved recognition. If it's not recognition that you're after, remember that you can always remain anonymous.

Charitable giving can also be win-win. The elderly aunt of one of our colleagues was struggling to take care of her home. It was a burden physically and emotionally. She made the decision to move into an assisted living facility. In her will, she had already provided that her home be given to a local college. But she was concerned about leaving her house empty and uncared for after she moved because the local college wouldn't receive the house until she died. We encouraged her to give her home to the college now. It benefited all involved. The aunt was relieved of a huge burden and received a big income tax deduction. The charity was able to begin using the property sooner rather than later.

You may have heard about a conservation easement. This is an easement on real property that restricts the uses of the property. It's a means of preserving "green space" in rapidly developing areas. The gift of a conservation easement may be a charitable contribution, and it's definitely a wonderful way to ensure that your favorite outdoor spot is preserved.

Some of the other creative charitable opportunities involve trusts and gift annuities. Charitable remainder annuity trusts (CRATs) or charitable remainder unitrusts (CRUTs) are trusts in which you or another person named by you receives the income from a trust during life. At death, the trust assets pass to the charity named in the trust. This is another win-win situation. You benefit during life. You also receive an income tax deduction for the current value of the trust remainder that will pass to the charity in the future. Even better, if you contribute low-basis assets (such as a stock that you bought for $5 a share that's now worth $100 a share) to the trust, you can sell them without incurring a capital gains tax. This can also be a beneficial means to increase cash flow for certain individuals. If you sell the stock, you might have to pay capital gains tax.

A charitable lead trust (CLT) provides an opposite benefit. With a CLT, the charity of your choice receives all of the income from a trust for a certain amount of time—let's say 10 years. At the end of the term, the trust assets, also called the **remainder**, pass to your named beneficiaries. You receive an income tax deduction for the income interest given to the charity. Unless you name yourself as the remainder beneficiary, there might be a taxable gift for the value of the remainder.

Because CRATs, CRUTs, and CLTs can be administratively burdensome, many charities offer to administer these trusts and also offer pooled income funds and charitable gift annuities. A pooled income fund allows for the donations of many donors to be pooled together to take advantage of certain investment opportunities. Each donor receives income from the fund based on the size of his or her donation. This is a great option for smaller donations. A charitable gift annuity is similar. A donor gives cash or securities to the charity, which invests the funds and provides a fixed income payment back to the donor (or another individual) for life. The benefit of pooled income funds and charitable gift annuities is that someone else is worrying about the details. Talk to your favorite charities. They'll be *more* than happy to discuss giving opportunities with you.

If you're concerned about having sufficient funds to care for yourself during life, you may want to postpone charitable giving until death. A charitable donation can be made in your will or trust. It can be a specific amount (such as $1,000) or a specific item (let's say a valuable painting). You can also establish one of the charitable trusts we discussed earlier for a spouse or another person at your passing.

The Famously Charitable

William Shakespeare gave "tenn poundes" to the "poore of Stratford." The father of our country, George Washington, endowed a university in Washington, D.C. (now known as George Washington University). Benjamin Franklin left his books to the City of Philadelphia, along with funds to the city of Boston for free schools. Babe Ruth left 10 percent of his estate to The Babe Ruth Foundation for underprivileged youth.

Individual retirement arrangements or other retirement benefits are terrific assets to pass to a charity. Why? At death, the IRA (Roth or traditional) could be subject to estate or inheritance tax. You'll also have to pay income tax if you take out a traditional IRA as a lump sum distribution. Add estate and inheritance taxes together, and your beneficiary could get as little as 20 cents on the dollar. If you pass your assets to charity instead of a beneficiary, the charity receives the entire account, tax free, and your estate receives a charitable deduction. We think of it as a bigger bang for your charitable buck.

If you want to benefit several charities and are interested in making a significant contribution, you can contribute to a community trust or start your own foundation. Establishing your own foundation provides you the opportunity to control all aspects of your charitable contributions. You control how the foundation's assets are invested. You also control which organizations receive benefits from your foundation. Your loved ones can become members of the foundation's board and learn the importance of philanthropy. A foundation, though, can be expensive to establish and requires many IRS and other filings. Alternatively, there are community trusts located throughout the country. Community trusts are often nonprofit organizations that may act as administrator of your contribution. You direct how the funds are distributed. This allows you to benefit a variety of organizations without the headache of establishing your own foundation. Either way, you're providing for others while maintaining control of decisions related to your contributions. Just remember, you can't change your mind—these donations are irrevocable.

Whether you choose to benefit a charitable organization, your children, or someone else, you're giving a piece of yourself. Take pride in what you do for others. But also make sure your wishes are effectively carried out. Planning well can take your good intentions and make them better. What more could you wish for?

Estate Planning Wishes

- Decide who needs your help—family, friends, or foundations.
- Decide what help your family, friends, or foundations need.
- Decide when and how to help.

15

Estate Planning Wills: Testaments, Trusts, and Other Tools

Before we talk of writing wills, we want to remind you that estate planning is necessary to ensure that your wants, wishes, and wills are carried out. With that said, your estate planning should be all about you: what *you* want, what *you* wish for, and what *you* decide. It shouldn't be based on the expectations of family members, the influence of friends, or what someone is "supposed to get." Before any client signs a will, we ask, in part, "do you make, publish, and declare this to be your Last Will and Testament, do you do so of your own free will, and are you not under any undue influence?" Your estate plan should be your will and your will alone.

As we like to remind our clients and patients, an inheritance is a gift, not an entitlement. If you recall only one thing as you read through this chapter and begin to make your plans, remember that every determination is your decision and your decision alone. Harold Ivan Smith noted in his book *Finding Your Way to Say Goodbye,*

Dying is about making choices. Good choices. Tough choices. Necessary choices. Soul-testing and soul-trying choices.

Your choices.

As we explained in Chapter 13, "Estate Planning Wants: Purpose, Preparation, and Protection," if you die without a will, the state decides who receives your assets. Take the time to prepare a will and other estate planning documents and make the choice yourself. You can select anyone: your spouse, your children, your best friend, your partner, your favorite niece or nephew, or charities. You can treat beneficiaries equally or not. You can also choose to exclude someone as a beneficiary. Don't be swayed by a sense of obligation or let others influence you or "guilt" you into something that you don't want to do. Again, it doesn't matter what you decide as long as it's *your* decision!

Explaining Your Decision

When preparing your will, some of you may worry that someone will feel hurt or slighted if he or she isn't listed as a beneficiary, executor, or trustee. Usually, if you've selected one person over another, there's a reason. If you're not comfortable discussing your decisions now, explain your thought process in a letter or note that accompanies your will. For example, "I decided that Pearl should serve as executor because she understands financial matters, is very organized, and has been helping with my finances for several years."

A Guide to Last Wills and Testaments

As noted earlier, many aspects of estate planning are dictated by your state of residence. We'll talk more about this in a bit, but first let's talk about some basics.

First, what exactly is a **will**? It's a document that, as defined in *Webster's New Collegiate Dictionary*, is a "legal declaration of a person's mind as to the manner in which he would have his property or estate disposed of after his death." Note that the definition says "legal declaration," not legal document. Although you don't have to get a lawyer to prepare your will, we suggest that you do. Why? Well, it isn't to drum up work for our colleagues. It's because wills are complicated. A will isn't just a standard form. It needs to be personalized to accurately reflect your wishes on everything from how estate taxes and debts are paid, to the powers of your executor or personal representative, to who takes care of your kids. And the procedure for signing a will to ensure it's valid—for example, how many witnesses must be present—varies from state to state. If you're going to the trouble of writing your will, you want to be sure it's going to be accepted by the courts. While we recommend planning your estate with the help of a knowledgeable lawyer, if cost is an issue and you can't get help from your local legal aid office, ask an attorney to review any will prepared using computer forms or samples from a stationary shop.

What's a Holographic Will?

A **holographic will** is written entirely in the handwriting of the person making the will and is signed, but is not witnessed or notarized. Some states recognize holographic wills. Others do not.

Many wills begin by providing that all of your debts, taxes, and expenses be paid by your estate. Your debts would include medical and credit card bills but would exclude mortgage debt (which would remain with the mortgaged real estate) unless you specify otherwise. Expenses are the costs associated with dying, such as funeral expenses, legal and accounting fees, and probate fees. Estate and inheritance taxes can be treated two ways. You can provide that your estate pay all of the taxes. Alternatively, you can provide that the taxes be split among your beneficiaries on a **pro rata** basis. Pro rata means that a 25 percent beneficiary pays 25 percent of any taxes and a 5 percent beneficiary pays 5 percent of any taxes. How the taxes are paid can be especially important if some of your assets are passing by beneficiary designation or joint tenancy. These assets pass without regard to your will; however, any taxes due should be paid as you direct in your will. Your attorney or accountant can advise you in deciding what's best for your particular circumstances.

We talked in Chapter 13 about how certain assets might be owned at your death—for example, joint tenancy assets, individually owned assets, and assets with a beneficiary designation. Now, let's talk about the different categories of individual assets that you might own: tangible personal property, real property, and intangible property. **Tangible personal property** is everything you can touch and feel, such as cars, jewelry, sports equipment, paintings, knick-knacks, and furniture. **Real property** is land and whatever is found on the land, whether it's a home, warehouse, or crops. **Intangible personal property** is everything else: stocks, bonds, and cash, for instance.

You may have heard of the term **community property**. Property obtained during marriage in one of the nine community property states (Arizona, California, Idaho, Louisiana, Nevada, New Mexico, Texas, Washington, and Wisconsin) is owned by both the husband and the wife, each spouse owning "an undivided one-half interest" in the entire asset. In Alaska, you can elect that your property be treated as community property. At death, the surviving spouse receives one-half of the community property; the spouse who has died may dispose of his or her share by will.

Who Can Write a Will?

Any competent person over the age of 18 can sign a will. A competent adult can understand information, evaluate choices, make decisions, and communicate his or her wishes.

When you're writing your will, be sure to remember your personal possessions. If we've learned one thing over the years, it's that dividing the personal property of a recently departed loved one can be a tinderbox of emotion. Some of the worst family disagreements are about the "stuff"—the silver, the photographs, and the old chipped mugs—that belonged to a beloved relative. Abigail, age 42, has vivid memories of hurt feelings and family unrest when her grandmother's will failed to address family "heirlooms," especially since there were supposedly many verbal promises of who was to receive what piece of jewelry.

Stephanie's Saga: Beware of Mysterious Lists

Planning ahead and making lists of "who gets what" could save your loved ones from engaging in a bitter family battle, which is exactly what happened to Stephanie, age 42. Within hours of her mother's death, Stephanie's sister-in-law Kelly presented her with a list. Days earlier, Kelly claimed that she had helped Stephanie's mother write a list of her personal property and who she wanted to receive her "loot." The list was in Kelly's handwriting and never signed by Stephanie's mother. And, at the time, Stephanie's mom was heavily medicated. Not surprisingly, Kelly's name appeared frequently on that list. Although it seems unlikely that the list was the intent of Stephanie's mother, Kelly's husband was the executor of the estate and influenced by Kelly, who demanded that the list be followed. For Stephanie, it's been an uphill battle involving lawyers and potential litigation. Although the executor finally woke up to what was happening, it was too late to prevent Stephanie's heartache and headaches.

So what do you do? First, don't make oral promises. This will help prevent "he said/she said" arguments. Second, make a written list, and be specific! The list should be in your own handwriting. Fully describe each item (for example, instead of writing "my ring," write "my ring with two sapphires and one diamond set in platinum") and the full name of the person to receive it. Our beloved (and very organized!) Aunt Mary left handwritten tags attached to jewelry and other heirlooms with the full name of the individual to receive each precious item. The items you list, however, don't have to be worth a lot of money. Sentimental value counts, too. We've seen knock-down drag out fights over Beanie Babies. A great deal of emotion can be attached to certain possessions, so the more direction you provide, the less conflict there should be. As the workbook titled *Who Gets Grandma's Yellow Pie Plate* notes,

> *Planning ahead allows for more choices, the opportunity for communication, and fewer misunderstandings and conflicts.*

In some states, your will may make reference to a memorandum you leave regarding your personal property. Check with your attorney to be sure any list you leave will be effective, and if not, ask that your list be added to your will. Be sure that language is included stating that any disputes are to be resolved by your executor or personal representative.

Some individuals take the opportunity to give special belongings to loved ones while they're still alive, especially if they're not using them anymore. This has two benefits. First, you can watch your loved one enjoy the item while you're alive. Second, there's less to fight about after you've passed. And if you think it's something no one wants, get rid of it! Believe us, no one needs 40 empty mayonnaise jars. Or even better, join the eBay craze and sell your stuff online or at a garage sale. You'll have some fun and might just make a few dollars. Leaving a house full of junk that needs to be cleaned up puts an even greater burden on the shoulders of your loved ones. Just ask Stephanie, age 42, who filled five three-ton dumpsters with junk when she emptied her mother's house.

With that said, we'll also admit that we each have basements full of, well, stuff, that we keep saying we're going to clean out but never do. It's because we simply can't face such an overwhelming task. So we've learned to make the chore manageable. Instead of saying that we have to clean out the whole basement, we create mini-tasks. For example, this week we'll sift through two shelves of old magazines or take one pile of clothes to goodwill. We don't expect you to jump up after reading this and run to clean out your closets. But we do hope you'll think about how your actions will help your heirs. And hey, as we noted earlier, if you can make a few bucks by selling your stuff, that should be incentive enough!

Do I Have to List Everything?

We agree, there is no way that any list or memorandum you leave with your will can cover every possible thing that you own. So leave instructions as to how all remaining items should be divided. Here are a few ideas:

- **Drawing straws**—Each beneficiary draws a straw. The individual with the longest straw selects the first remaining item of personal property. The next longest straw holder goes second, and so on until all wanted items have been selected. We suggest that this be done with only the beneficiaries present. Unfortunately, we've found that the presence of in-laws and nosy friends can bring negativity to the process.

- **Wish lists**—Each beneficiary prepares a wish list of personal items and provides it to your executor or personal representative. If no one else wants a particular item, it passes to the person who requested it. Items requested by more than one individual are then divided by drawing straws.

- **Equal values**—Have the personal items appraised. Divide the total value of the appraised items by the number of beneficiaries. (For example, if the personal property is valued at $10,000 and there are four beneficiaries, each beneficiary is entitled to items worth a total of $2,500.) Have the beneficiaries draw straws. As soon as a beneficiary has reached his or her "value quota," he or she is prohibited from selecting additional objects.

- **Sell it all**—If you're concerned that your beneficiaries will do nothing but fight, direct that all of your personal property be sold. Whatever money is made from the sale can be added to your residuary estate and distributed according to your will.
- **Give, give, give**—Provide that any items of value (antiques and paintings) be donated to a museum. Have all clothing and personal items given to local charities. Arrangements can be made for furniture and electronics to be donated to local or national organizations.

Now that we've taken care of your personal possessions, let's move on to the rest of your estate. Before you decide who receives the majority of your assets, you may want to leave some small or specific gifts to individuals or charities. These are referred to as either specific bequests or specific devises. For example, you may want to leave $1,000 to your church, synagogue, or mosque or $10,000 to your college or university. Some individuals choose to leave small remembrances to younger relatives—let's say, $500 to each grandchild. There is no dollar amount limit or requirement that a bequest or devise be made in cash. For instance, vacant land may be left to a land conservancy charity or shares of a particular stock to a sister. Bequests and devises provide an opportunity to remember an individual or organization, but they are not required.

What About Spot and Fluffy?

Can you leave money to man's best friend in a will? The answer is no. But there are other options. You can leave a bequest to the person who you've asked to "adopt" your cats, to be used for their care. Alternatively, you can leave a bequest to a local animal shelter with a request that some of the funds be used to find your Golden Retriever a new home. Some folks set up trusts to benefit their four-legged friends. Talk to your attorney for additional ideas.

After all expenses, debts, and taxes are paid, your personal property distributed, and any specific bequests or devises made, what's left is your residuary estate—in other words, all your other possessions. Unless you leave your real estate to a specific individual as a devise, it becomes part of your residuary estate. This is where the planning comes in.

Family Planning

We often think of estate planning as being a family plan. Discuss the subject with your loved ones. Listen to what they have to say. Many of our single clients want to leave their estates to their parents. We usually advise against this to avoid possible double taxation in the event of deaths that occur close together. If your daughter, Linda, has been very successful, she may ask you to skip her and leave everything to her children. Should any potential beneficiaries be disabled, find out what planning has been done on their behalf to avoid jeopardizing their eligibility for government benefits. Families can work together to find a plan that benefits all branches of the family tree.

The planning part of your will begins with whom you want to receive your residuary estate. It can be one person or charity, many people or many charities, or some combination. Most married folks leave their estates to their spouse, or if their spouse isn't alive, to their children. If you have several children, you can decide whether your estate gets divided among your children who are living (**per capita**) or, if a child has died, whether his or her share will pass to his or her children (**per stirpes**). See the following sidebar for information on these legal terms. If you don't have children and aren't married, you can name your siblings or maybe nieces and nephews. Perhaps you have a partner whom you want to benefit from your estate.

Legalese 101

We'll admit it—lawyers love using fancy legal terms. Here are explanations of a few phrases you'll likely encounter:

Irrevocable—A legal document that can't be changed or revoked.

Revocable—A legal document that can be changed, amended, or cancelled.

Issue—All individuals born of a common ancestor. Your children, grandchildren, and great-grandchildren (and so on) are your *issue*. Also referred to as **descendants**.

Per capita—Division of an estate among a single branch of the family tree, share and share alike. If you leave your estate to your children per capita and one of your children has already died, that child's share will be split among your living children.

Per stirpes—Division of an estate among all branches of a family tree. If you leave your estate to your children per stirpes and one of your children has already died, that child's share will pass to his or her children. Also referred to as **by representation**.

The way you divide your estate is up to you. It can be in equal shares or by percentages. Try to avoid using dollar amounts because some inequity can result depending on changes in the size of your estate at your death. Once you've determined who you want your beneficiaries to be and how much you want them to receive, the next decision is how they receive the funds.

If your beneficiary is an adult, you may want him or her to receive a share of your estate outright—in other words, with no strings attached. Or maybe you prefer someone's inheritance to be held in trust. Married individuals usually choose to leave their estates outright to their significant other. However, this might not be the best plan for two reasons.

What's a Trust?

A **trust** is property that is managed by a trustee for another person's benefit—the beneficiary. It's a method to safeguard assets for the beneficiary.

Let's say that you have children from a prior marriage or relationship. If you leave everything to your current spouse, your children could end up empty handed after your spouse dies. Of course, your spouse may promise to provide for your children. But that's an unenforceable promise. And although he or she might have the best intentions, countless things could happen to those funds (such as bankruptcy or poor investments). In this situation, we would suggest placing the funds into a trust for your spouse's benefit. Your spouse would receive the income from the trust plus additional funds if he or she is sick or needs additional support. Later, when your spouse dies, the remaining trust assets would be distributed to your children (or whomever you want). A trust for a spouse allows you to take care of your better half but still provide for your family.

Tax planning is another reason that you might want to consider a trust for a spouse. Under current federal law, we all have a certain amount that we can pass to anyone free of federal estate tax ($2,000,000 in 2007). There is an unlimited deduction for assets passing to a spouse (unless your spouse isn't a U.S. citizen). If you give all of your money to your spouse when you die, there will be no taxes at your death. However, the amount you can pass tax free to other loved ones has been lost. Here's an example. You and your spouse each have $2,000,000. You die and leave your spouse all of your assets. Your spouse now has $4,000,000. When your spouse dies, he or she has an estate valued at $4,000,000 but can only pass $2,000,000 free of federal estate tax. The result—lots of taxes. If you had left your

$2,000,000 in a trust for your significant other, it wouldn't be included in his or her estate and together you would have passed $4,000,000 tax free to your heirs. No taxes versus lots of tax. We know what we'd choose.

Your plan doesn't have to be all outright or all in trust. You can create a customized plan with some assets passing outright and some being held in trust. A trust can be for life or a term of years. There are countless creative options. Talk to your counselor for ideas.

As we noted earlier, money you leave to a spouse who isn't a U.S. citizen doesn't qualify for the unlimited marital deduction. However, there is an option to avoid federal estate tax on funds you leave to your non-U.S. spouse. It's called a qualified domestic trust. This type of trust, which requires a U.S. citizen or bank to serve as trustee, provides income to your spouse for his or her lifetime. Any principal distributions of the trust assets, though, could be subject to tax.

Because the tax laws are changing, many practitioners now suggest that a married couple consider "disclaimer" wills. With a disclaimer will, you leave everything to your spouse, outright and free from trust. However, when you pass away, your spouse can sign a disclaimer that results in a trust being created for his or her benefit. Why do this? It allows your spouse to evaluate the current tax laws, his or her health, and the value of your assets at the time you die. Bottom line: It's a flexible plan that may be worth considering.

We strongly suggest that you establish trusts for underage children to provide for their education and care while they're young. If you're leaving significant funds, you may want to require that the money remain in trust until your kids reach certain ages, with principal distributions at ages such as 25, 30, and 35. Maybe you have a beneficiary who is disabled. In that event, we urge you to consult an attorney specializing in estate and disability planning. Or maybe you have a son-in-law who you don't trust and want to protect your daughter's inheritance. If you place the funds in trust for her benefit, your son-in-law will be unable to access the funds. There is much that can be done to protect your loved ones.

What's the Difference Between a Will and a Trust?

A will states how you want your assets to be distributed when you die. A trust holds property for the benefit of another. A trust can be established during life (an **inter vivos trust**) or at death (a **testamentary trust**).

Some individuals try to exert what's called dead hand control by including certain contingencies in a will or trust. For example, we've read wills that require a beneficiary to attend a particular college or marry into a certain religious faith before receiving a bequest. One trust stated that a beneficiary would not receive trust income if he engaged in "conduct unbecoming a gentleman." We think this may be going a bit too far. We also advise against using your will as a weapon. We're talking about making promises of inheritances in return for certain behavior or a threat to "cut someone out of your will" if he or she does something you don't like. These actions are not only emotionally destructive to your beneficiary; but they can also be grounds for litigation after you've died.

Remember, you can always exclude an individual from receiving benefits under your will. If you want to exclude a particular person, we recommend specifically mentioning this in your will. Include a statement that says something like, "I specifically exclude my grandson, Gordon Golddigger, from my will and intend that he receive no benefit from my estate in any manner." This way, Mr. Golddigger can't argue that he was mistakenly omitted from the will. There may be a temptation for some to exclude a spouse from receiving under the will. In many states, a spouse is entitled to an automatic elective share under the will if he or she is omitted. Talk to your attorney— there may be a better option for you.

Because it's part of our job to cover every possible eventuality, we also suggest including a so-called **common disaster** clause in the unlikely event that all of your beneficiaries die before or at the same time as you. We don't mean to make light of such tragedies, but we often refer to this as the family vacation plane crash. Although such a scenario is unlikely, you still need to plan for it. Many of our clients pick nieces or nephews to receive their assets in this case. Others pick charitable organizations. If you don't make a provision for this scenario, the laws of intestacy will apply.

Once you've determined how to distribute your estate, you need to decide who will administer it. This is your executor or personal representative. The job of an executor is usually completed within a year or two. Your executor can be a family member or friend. It can be a financial institution with trust powers. Or it can be a combination of the two. An executor is entitled to commissions, which are usually at a rate defined by your state's law. If you pick a financial institution, you may be able to negotiate a different rate.

The Executor

I had a friend who died and he
On Earth so loved and trusted me
That when he quit this worldly shore
He made me his executor.
He asked me through my natural life
To guard the interest of his wife;
To see that everything was done
Both for his daughter and his son.
I have his money to invest,
And though I try my level best
To do that wisely, I'm advised.
My judgment often is criticized.
His widow, once so calm and meek,
Comes, hot with rage, three times a week
And rails at me because I must,
To keep my oath, appear unjust.

His children hate the sight of me,
Although their friend I've tried to be,
And every relative declares
I interfere with his affairs.
Now when I die I'll never ask
A friend to carry such a task.
I'll spare him all such anguish sore
And leave a hired executor

—Edgar Guest

The job of a trustee can last much longer, especially if you have young beneficiaries. The trustee manages the trust, much like a small business, as long as it lasts. If the trustee is given a great deal of discretion, you'll want someone who understands your intentions and goals. In this circumstance, you should consider the age and health of the individual or individuals that you name. And be sure to include a provision for successors. If you're establishing a trust for your spouse, you may want him or her to serve with another individual or a bank or trust company.

When selecting your executor and trustee, you don't need to pick a financial genius. You also don't have to select someone who lives locally. If you've decided on an individual, we suggest selecting someone who is prudent enough to ask for help from lawyers, accountants, and financial planners. Consider your circumstances. Is there likely to be a fight or animosity among your beneficiaries? Do your children hate their stepmother? If that's the case, you may want a neutral financial institution or third party to serve. In selecting a financial institution, Joseph Gazdalski, vice president of the Glenmede Trust Company of Philadelphia, recommends that you look for the following:

stability, peace of mind, identifiable costs, competitive investment returns, ease of communication, and most of all preservation of family harmony when considering a corporate fiduciary...comfort is key.

If your attorney suggests that he or she serve as your executor or trustee, look elsewhere. We believe that it's a conflict of interest for your counselor to serve as your fiduciary (unless, of course, you ask this person to serve or he or she is a close personal friend or family member).

Fiduciary Duty

Any individual or institution acting on your behalf, whether it's as an executor, trustee, or guardian, has a fiduciary duty to exercise care and responsibility. In other words, there's a legal obligation to act with trust and good faith. Be sure that your will contains a statement that you don't want any of your fiduciaries to be required to post a **surety bond**—a kind of insurance policy. This is an expense that you can avoid.

For many people, the hardest part of writing a will is naming a guardian for their young children. It's an emotional and extraordinarily difficult decision. But it's also one of the most important reasons to have a will. You may love your parents or siblings but not want them to raise your kids. Or maybe you want to head off what you anticipate would be a battle among the grandparents if something happened to both you and your spouse. Not only should you select a guardian, but you should also select one or two successor guardians. In selecting the guardian, we usually advise against naming a married couple. If you want your sister and brother-in-law to serve as guardians, only name your sister in the event they divorce. Or include language in your will that specifies your sister will serve as guardian if she and her husband split up. A guardian can only be named in your will.

Who Should Be the Guardian of My Children?

First, we want to clear up one myth: A child's godparents do not automatically become that child's guardians if you die. A godfather or godmother is a religious role only and has no legal responsibilities or entitlements. With that said, we recommend selecting a guardian based on who will raise your child as you would. It doesn't have to be a relative. It doesn't have to be someone who can afford one more mouth to feed. Focus on who will love your child and who shares your beliefs and values.

In addition to naming a guardian, many individuals include language in their will discussing their hopes for their children. We've seen language requiring that children be allowed to visit with other relatives, or requesting that the appointed guardian travel with the children to a favorite destination, or encouraging the guardian to arrange for particular educational opportunities. Alternatively, you can prepare a Letter of Guidance to be presented to a guardian in the event of your death.

Guardian Letter of Guidance

We all have strong feelings about how our children should be raised. We have goals and dreams for their futures. Share your thoughts with your guardian in a Letter of Guidance. Tell this person if religious education is important. Explain that your child's attendance at camp each summer should be a priority. Let your guardian know that you want your kids to take foreign language lessons as early as possible. If you don't write it down, how will this person know what you intended?

We understand how difficult it is to select a guardian. However, not selecting someone would be worse if your families end up fighting, forcing a court to decide who should be your child's guardian. So make your decision, and put it in writing.

The rest of a will generally contains the powers of your executor and trustee and a lot of boilerplate legalese. There's often a provision stating that you don't want there to be a public accounting of your estate. This keeps things private. Review these provisions carefully, and make sure they're satisfactory.

You should only sign one original will, not multiple copies. Your will should include a statement revoking all prior wills. Once your will is signed, do not write on it or make notes on the original. Likewise, don't unbind the original or remove the staples. Your will should be kept in a safe spot, perhaps with the attorney who drafted it or in a firebox in your home. Make sure your loved ones know where the original is. If you have an old will, revoke it by ripping it up, burning it, or writing "Revoked" across the front.

Procrastination Nation

Americans may be the leaders in science, entrepreneurship, and medicine, but we get a failing grade on preparation. Studies suggest that only 30 percent of Americans have Last Wills and Testaments. The same is true for Living Wills, as well as other estate planning documents. One report indicated that only 10 percent of the individuals who died on 9/11 had wills. Having worked with families of the terrorist attack victims, we know firsthand the anguish caused by not having a valid will. Stop procrastinating and just do it!

A Guide to Trusts

Think about the word *trust*. The dictionary defines it as "assured reliance on the character, ability, strength, or truth of someone or something." When you create a trust, that's exactly what you're doing: placing your assets with someone or some institution that you can trust to safeguard them, either for yourself or another.

If I Have a Trust, Do I Need a Will?

Yes! Even if you've established a trust and transferred all of your assets into it, we still suggest that you have a will. Why? There could be one tiny asset that was never transferred into the trust that can wreak havoc on even the best-laid plan. Such problems can often be solved with a will. If you have a trust, you can provide that your will "pour" any remaining assets into the trust at your death. And remember: If you have underage children, you also need a will to name a guardian.

As we mentioned previously, there are two general types of trusts: a trust created during your lifetime (an inter vivos trust) and a trust established at your death (a testamentary trust). We also talked about some of the different trusts you might create under your will for a spouse or children.

So what kind of trust might you set up while you're still alive? As we explained in Chapter 13, in some states probate can be a nightmare. To avoid it, residents are advised to set up trusts during their lifetimes. Such a trust is often called a **Living Trust**, a **grantor trust**, or a **revocable trust**. It provides that, as long as you're living, you receive all of the income and as much of the principal, or **corpus**, of the trust as you want or need. The trust is revocable, so you can change or terminate it at any time. You can be the trustee of your Living Trust. We like to think of a Living Trust as simply a different name for your assets. Instead of the assets being owned by you, the assets are now owned by your trust. Nothing has really changed, except the way the assets are titled.

When you die, your Living Trust becomes irrevocable. Your successor trustee then follows the terms of your trust, which outlines how to distribute your assets. This includes provisions like those found in a will. For example, you can provide for several small gifts to be made to family members, friends, or your favorite charities. You then provide for the division of the remainder of your trust assets. You can also establish trusts for beneficiaries. Unlike a will, a Living Trust does not require probate. There's no need to prove it's valid because you take care of that while you're alive. In other words, your Living Trust becomes your will with the added benefit of avoiding probate.

Your estate planning isn't limited to providing for your loved ones at death. You can set up trusts today and make contributions to them during your life. One popular trust is for a child or grandchild, perhaps to pay for college. There are also trusts for disabled individuals, which provide benefits to a disabled person without jeopardizing his or her government benefits. We see trusts established to own real estate or other specific assets. There are charitable trusts, asset protection trusts, insurance trusts, personal residence trusts, and many other options. Converse with your counselor to see if you should consider one of them.

A Guide to Other Estate Planning Tools

Volumes have been written about all the other estate planning tools that are available to direct your estate and to save on potential taxes. A detailed discussion of these mechanisms is beyond the scope of this book, but we'll give you a quick overview.

When you think of life insurance, we bet you only think about the group life policy you get through work or a simple term policy. You know, the 20-year term policy you buy in case you die when your kids are young? Well, life insurance has grown up. There are myriad ways to use life insurance not only as an investment opportunity but also as an estate planning tool. A joint and survivor life insurance policy insures two individuals, usually a married couple, and pays out on the second death. This reduces the cost of the policy. Of course, because insurance is an estate asset if the insured owns and controls it, the policy should be owned by an irrevocable life insurance trust or someone else, such as your kids, to avoid additional taxes that might be due on your passing. Ronald J. Greenberg of the Greenberg and Rapp Financial Group, Inc., recommends talking with a financial professional for a review of your current insurance situation. To find a credentialed professional in your area, go to http://financialpro.org.

Long-Term Care and Disability Insurance

Long-term care insurance provides benefits that can pay for home, personal, or nursing home care, as well as other services for people in assisted living facilities or adult day care centers. Every policy covers varied services for different lengths of time and dollar amounts. Long-term care insurance is expensive—so it's not right for everyone. Disability insurance replaces your income (or some part of your income) if you're unable to work because of illness or injury. Some employers offer disability insurance. Check with an insurance broker or financial advisor to find out if these types of insurance are right for you.

If you own a small business, planning for your death is especially critical. You need to be concerned about who will take the reins when you die (succession planning), as well as the transfer of your interest in the business. Perhaps you have a partner who will want to buy your share or a key employee who should be given the opportunity. A buy/sell agreement is one of the documents to consider.

Earlier in this chapter, we talked about giving away personal belongings while you're still alive. The same holds true for money and other assets. Under current law, every year you can give $12,000 per person to as many people as you want without paying a gift tax. (This is called the annual exclusion from gift tax and is indexed annually for inflation.) The gift isn't considered income to the recipient, either. If you're married and your better half agrees, you can double that amount to $24,000. The gift can be in cash or other property. (Check with your accountant, though—there could be capital gains tax ramifications to giving away securities and other assets.) You can make gifts outright or in trust. There are Section 529 plans (tax-deferred savings available in some states) to save for education as well as other custodial accounts for minors.

Of course, you can also make gifts in excess of the $12,000 annual exclusion from gift tax. Any amount you give in excess of $12,000 is considered a taxable gift. Although gifts in excess of this amount are taxable, you don't actually have to pay a gift tax. As of 2007, you can make gifts of up to $1,000,000 during your lifetime without having to write a check to the IRS. How does this work? Well, the total taxable gifts that you make during your life reduce the exclusion from federal estate tax available at your death. We'll give you an example. You make a $112,000 gift to your favorite nephew Ned in 2007. The annual exclusion amount of the gift is $12,000, making the taxable gift $100,000. If you die in 2007, you no longer have $2,000,000 that you can pass tax free—you have $1,900,000. There is no cap on payments of tuition made directly to an educational institution or medical payments made directly to a provider. For some, gifting during life is better. Your loved ones can use the funds now, and you can remove potentially appreciable assets from your estate.

Finally, the charitable giving options discussed in Chapter 14, "Estate Planning Wishes: Caring for Family, Friends, and Foundations," are wonderful for estate planning. Not only does charitable giving benefit others, but it also has the possibility of reducing death taxes on your passing.

In Chapter 9, "Medical-Legal Wills: Directives, Definitions, and Discussions," we discussed at length the importance of having a Power of Attorney, Health Care or Medical Proxy, and Living Will. If you haven't already signed these documents, discuss them with your lawyer when you're reviewing your estate planning.

Estate Planning Decisions

The following is a list of important estate planning decisions to be made:

- Name and address of the individual or institution to serve as executor, as well as at least two successor executors.
- Name and address of the individual or institution to serve as trustee, as well as at least two successor trustees.
- Name and address of the guardian of your minor or disabled children, as well as at least two successor guardians.
- List of any small or specific bequests or devises. Include full legal names and addresses of the beneficiaries.
- Beneficiaries of your estate and how you would like them to receive their inheritance. Include full legal names and addresses. Tell your attorney if any beneficiary is a minor, is disabled, or is not a U.S. citizen.
- Provisions for your common disaster clause. Include full legal names and addresses.
- Name and address of your agent under a Power of Attorney, as well as two successor agents.
- Name and address of your health care representative under a Health Care Proxy, as well as two successor health care representatives.
- Your wants and wishes at the end of life, and any religious language to be contained in your Living Will.

The more information you can provide your attorney at your initial meeting, the shorter the meeting and the smaller the fee.

Once you've signed your documents, we recommend reviewing your plan at least every five years, or after any major life events, such as deaths, divorces, marriages, or births, or if you have a significant change in your assets. We also suggest that you keep your documents in a safe place, such as a readily accessible firebox. This protects your invaluable documents not only in the event of fire, but should you have to evacuate quickly, you'll only have a single box to grab in case you have to run for cover!

We recognize that we've provided you with a great deal of information in this section. Think of the information as tools to help you create an estate plan customized to your wants, wishes, and wills. Use these tools as you consult with your advisors. Together, you can build the perfect plan for you and your loved ones.

Estate Planning Wills

- Write your Last Will and Testament.
- Establish trusts.
- Select executors, trustees, and guardians.
- Write Letters of Guidance if you have minor or disabled children.

Section VI

The Wants, Wishes, and Wills of Your Legacy

When people who are facing the end of life consider their legacy, they often focus only on property and possessions. But your legacy is about so much more. It's the ideas, instructions, and intentions that you leave your loved ones. It's your personal history, your family tree, your favorite memories. It's the joys you've experienced, the sadness you've endured, and the accomplishments you've achieved. It's you and everything about you.

We all want to leave a part of ourselves behind when we depart this life. Some want to leave an invention or idea that benefits others. Some want to leave a legacy of lessons for those they love. Others are practical and simply want to make it easy on those left behind. In Chapter 16, "Legacy Wants: Providing Ideas, Intentions, and Instructions" we suggest writing letters of love, instructions, and intentions. We help you focus on your personal history, family tree, and information storage in Chapter 17, "Legacy Wishes: Assisting Family, Friends, and Future Generations to Remember." Lastly, in

Chapter 18, "Legacy Wills: Your Safety, Your Rights, and Your Records," we provide you with a summary of your rights as a patient and the importance of your personal records.

There is nothing to prevent you from preparing your legacy. You can choose to leave your legacy or not. We think, though, that it's a gift of yourself you'd regret not giving.

16

Legacy Wants: Providing Ideas, Instructions, and Intentions

We've talked a lot throughout this book about writing down your wants, wishes, and wills. The writing doesn't stop with formal legal documents. We also encourage you to write down your ideas, instructions, and intentions. In this chapter, we focus on each of these items. We explain the importance of sharing your love with your nearest and dearest. Next, we help you prepare a Letter of Instruction to guide your family and friends after your passing. Lastly, we discuss how you can take charge of your funeral plans to ensure that your intentions are carried out.

Although we strongly believe in providing these items for your loved ones, you should only do it if you're emotionally able. Based on our professional experiences and observations of our patients and clients, these actions can bring comfort to those facing the end of life, as well as their families. But if the subjects are too uncomfortable or upsetting, there's no harm in avoiding them.

A Guide to Letters and Lessons of Love

Later in this chapter, we discuss Letters of Instruction. These are business-like letters—who to call, what to do, where to start. Equally important are what we refer to as Letters and Lessons of Love. These are letters, videos, poems, or conversations that allow you to share your personal philosophies, hopes, dreams, and anything else that you think is important, with your loved ones.

In Jim Stovall's novel, *The Ultimate Gift*, a recently departed uncle leaves his nephew 12 months of lessons to teach him the importance of work, money, friends, learning, problems, family, laughter, dreams, giving, gratitude, each day, and love. Think of the lessons that you want to convey. Instead of waiting until you're gone, however, share these wonderful gifts now.

For some of you, these lessons may consist of practical information. When we were growing up, an elderly neighbor tried and tried to teach his wife how to manage the family finances, when to pay bills, how to balance their checkbook, and what information was required for their tax return. His wife refused to learn. Months later, when our neighbor died, his wife was unprepared. She hadn't written a check in 50 years, knew nothing about taxes, and was simply overwhelmed with life's day-to-day tasks. In addition to being grief stricken, she had the added stress of learning how to manage her own affairs. She kept repeating, "I should have listened."

We both grew up learning from our parents the value of education, both formal and informal. Today, we try to pass this lesson on to younger generations. We also benefited from travel and knowledge of other cultures. It certainly made us appreciate our country when we saw the poverty, destitution, and lack of freedom of others around the world, something we also try to share with those we care for. But these are our views and our views only. As we observe our friends and colleagues, we know that what's important to us isn't important to everyone. Some love all things sports—from baseball to soccer to games played on the gridiron. We see lessons taught about sportsmanship, teamwork, and drive. Our goal (yes, pun intended!) is to encourage you to identify what has meaning to you and to pass it on. It doesn't have to rival the teachings of the great philosophers. Simply share your thoughts, views, and desires in any way that works for you.

Some use these letters as a way to say goodbye—little notes of love and encouragement, sharing sentiments and sadness at the prospect of not being there when important future events take place, or small, poignant remembrances. We know of incredibly thoughtful parents who, knowing that death was imminent, took the time to write letters to their children to be opened on graduation days, wedding days, and special birthdays. Scrapbooks and albums are made highlighting special moments and joyous occasions. Others use videos to do the same thing. Make the time to have heart-to-heart conversations with your loved ones about everything from your investing and savings philosophies to your religious beliefs to the importance of hard work, or whatever it is that you believe in. Take every opportunity to say, "I love you." We know that it can take courage and a willingness to be vulnerable to share your feelings. Say it anyway. Your loved ones may know how you feel, but they still want to hear it.

Video Memorials

The terrorist attacks on September 11 left many small children without a mother or father. The friends of one family we know brought out a video camera and started filming. The result is a beautiful collection of recordings of loved ones remembering David, his strengths, his weaknesses, what made him a great guy, how much he loved his wife and kids, even the terrible jokes he told. It's a moving tribute to David that his kids can watch over and over to learn about their dad and why everyone loved him.

As we noted in Chapter 15, "Estate Planning Wills: Testaments, Trusts, and Other Tools," you may want to leave a Letter of Guidance for the guardian of your minor or disabled children. Use this letter as an opportunity to share your visions and dreams for your kids. Leave specific details as to what you hope will happen—that your child will learn to speak a second language, participate in particular religious events, spend time with a favorite cousin, or learn to play a musical instrument. You can be general or incredibly specific—it's up to you. Although this letter isn't binding, it provides direction to the person caring for your children. It will help your guardian as he or she raises your kids and teaches them about you.

The lessons you leave can be serious and helpful, but they can also be silly and fun. Try a combination of the two. It doesn't matter what you leave behind. They will be lessons of love because they came from you. They'll be something that, when you're gone, is irreplaceable.

A Guide to Letters of Instruction

As young teenagers, we both lost loved ones, including a much loved step-grandmother. In addition to fond memories of Ruth, there is one very vivid memory: the meticulous instructions that she left for her step-son. She included in her Letter of Instruction every detail—where she wanted to be buried (including location of the cemetery plot that she had already purchased), who should be called, what she wanted to wear, as well as information regarding safe deposit boxes and financial records. The burden this lifted from our family was immense. There was no worry or time wasted wondering "What would she want?" "Who should we call?" and "Where does she wish to be laid to rest?" Instead, our family was able to move quickly through the planning process, allowing more time to be spent with grieving friends and loved ones. Reflecting back, Ruth gave her stepson a gift greater than any monetary legacy. With her simple, handwritten Letter of Instruction, she gave him peace of mind—a gift that every family would be lucky to receive.

In contrast, we have encountered many people with an urn of cremated ashes in the back of a closet. The ashes sit there for years (in the case of one family member, for 13 years) because the now long-departed never provided instructions to his or her loved ones. So nothing is done as those left behind struggle with "What would Mom have wanted?" We doubt the hall closet would have been Mom's choice. We include this not to upset you but to encourage you to share your wishes with your family. If you're not comfortable discussing them, write a Letter of Instruction to be opened only after you pass.

If you're reading this book in an effort to help an ailing friend or family member, raising these questions isn't easy. We know. We confess that, despite working with families every day on such important subjects, we had not raised these issues with our own parents when we began writing this book. Why? Because they're in good health and, maybe like you, we didn't want to know the answers. But we gritted our teeth and asked. And now we're happy we did.

What should a Letter of Instruction include? We consider the Letter of Instruction to fall into three parts: your wants, wishes, and wills. Your wants should begin your Letter of Instruction. The first priority should be a list of friends and loved ones who should learn as soon as possible of your death. Include contact information or the location where this information may be found. Don't assume that your children, for example, will remember to call your favorite college roommate or your long-time pastor.

Your wants should also include information to be contained in your obituary as well as the newspapers that should receive notification of your death. If you recently moved to a new community, you may want your hometown paper, or other communities where you lived, to publish your obituary. Jeremy Pearce, obituary journalist for *The New York Times*, says a typical obituary includes your education, employment history, prizes and honors, surviving family members, and place of residence. This is just a beginning point. Also leave a list of items or facts that you'd like to have included. If you served with a particular military unit, for example, leave a list of the details for your family to give to the local newspaper. As part of a religion class in college, we were required to author our own obituaries. It was a difficult assignment, but it was incredibly thought provoking.

Next, your Letter of Instruction should include your wishes regarding your funeral, memorial service, or life celebration. Some individuals believe these details should be included in their Last Will and Testament. However, if a death occurs on a Friday evening, plans may need to be implemented long before the lawyer can be contacted and the will read to see what, if any, details are included. That's why we suggest leaving specific details in your Letter of Instruction. If you have not made the funeral plans yourself (see page **228**), the following information will be extraordinarily helpful to your loved ones:

- What is the name and contact information for the funeral director if funeral plans have been made or paid for?

- Have you made specific requests regarding your funeral in any legal documents? If so, make a note to your loved ones to contact your lawyer or tell them where these documents are located.

- Do you wish to be buried or cremated?

- If buried, do you already own a cemetery plot? If not, where would you like to be buried? Is there a family plot? If you're a veteran, there are many burial benefits you may be entitled to from the Veteran's Administration. Log onto www.va.gov for details.

- If you prefer cremation, how should your ashes be disposed of? Should they be buried or placed in a mausoleum? Or spread in a place of special memory?

- Do you want a full funeral celebration? Or a simple memorial service? If visitation is to take place, do you wish for an open or closed casket?

- Do you have any preferences regarding what you will wear or objects you might wish to be buried with (for example, jewelry, photographs, religious items)?

- If you prefer that charitable contributions be made in your honor instead of flowers, what organization do you choose to be the beneficiary of such remembrances?

- Do you have preferences for music, poems, religious passages, or speakers at the service in your honor?

- What information do you wish to have included in your obituary or death notice? What publications do you want to print the notice?

- Who would you like to have serve as pallbearers?

In the wills section of your Letter of Instruction, include all important contact and financial information. We suggest including the following:

- Name and telephone number of your attorney.
- Location of your original Last Will and Testament and other legal documents, including trust agreements, deeds, cemetery plot records, original stock certificates, and automobile or other vehicle titles.
- Name and telephone number of your accountant.
- Location of past income and gift tax returns.
- Name and telephone number of your financial advisor.

- Location of any safe deposit box, and the location of the key.

- List of all bank and brokerage accounts and account numbers.

- List of all life insurance and annuity policies, policy numbers, and whereabouts of the original policies.

- List of any organizations that may provide a death benefit, for example, social organizations, the Veteran's Administration, and unions.

- List of all employee benefits you receive and whether there may be a death benefit. Any contact information should also be included.

- Location of all account passwords or other access information, including your online service provider. (We've discovered it's next to impossible to terminate an online account without the necessary access information.)

- Location of any "hidden" items. This might include jewelry, sterling silver, or cash. Give your heirs a hint where to look.

Providing this information will save your loved ones countless hours of rummaging through drawers and file cabinets in an effort to accumulate this information. It will also prevent the loss of certain benefits because no one knew, for example, that your membership in the XYZ Club provides a small death benefit to members.

Keep your Letter of Instruction in a readily accessible location, such as an unlocked fire box, file cabinet, or nightstand drawer. We refer to it as the "important paper drawer." It's a place friends and family will know to look when needed. Alternatively, tell your children or best friend where to look. Don't place your Letter of Instruction in a safe deposit box since access is limited to bank hours and to the executor of your estate or cosignatory on the box. You may want to give copies to your loved ones today. If you're uncomfortable sharing the details of your Letter of Instruction at this time, at the very least let your loved ones know where it's located so it can be easily obtained when required.

Letter of Instruction Checklist

Funeral Instructions

- Wishes regarding burial or cremation
- Location of cemetery or mausoleum deed or ownership certificate
- Funeral home of choice (note if services have been prepaid)
- Attire
- Service preferences
- Pallbearers, if appropriate
- Obituary details
- Charitable contribution information (in lieu of flowers)

Contact Information

- Attorney
- Accountant
- Financial planner
- Insurance agent/broker
- Human resources/benefits manager
- Family members
- Friends
- Professional and social organizations
- Alumni associations

Important Information

- Safe deposit box location and key location
- Location of Last Will and Testament
- Location of insurance policies
- Location of deeds, titles and registrations
- Location of original stock certificates
- Location of valuables and keys
- Asset lists, account numbers, contact information
- Death benefits

A Guide to Funeral Planning

As surprising as it may seem, many terminally ill patients take great joy in planning their funerals. We have always been and remain consistently impressed by our friends, patients, and clients who have the strength and courage to make these plans to save their spouses and children the difficulty of decision making in a time of grief. Making these decisions can also provide the dying a sense of peace and control.

One individual in particular comes to mind. He was the father of one of our schoolmates. Although his death was anticipated, the end came sooner rather than later. Arriving at the local funeral home during the visitation hours, our classmate was greeting friends. Despite her grief, she looked stunning in a beautiful black dress, as did her sisters and her mother. She remarked that her father insisted that they buy new dresses to wear and model them for him weeks earlier. His funeral, he suggested, would be a celebration, and his "girls" should look the part. Not only did he select the music, the passages to be read, and the beer to be served at the post-funeral gathering, but our classmate's clever father selected a funeral home run by a family with several single sons beginning their careers in the family business. He wanted to play matchmaker even after his passing. While no romances flourished, each daughter was touched by her father's desire to see her happy and loved even after his death. He wanted the event to be a celebration. His wish was fulfilled.

For some, like Morrie Schwartz in Mitch Albom's bestselling book *Tuesdays with Morrie*, planning your own funeral also means attending your own funeral. Morrie planned his "living funeral" so that he could visit with friends, say goodbye, and enjoy their company one last time. Take the time to see long-distance friends while you're able. If you have the means, invite relatives from out of town to come to you so that you can enjoy their company. Although this unusual manner of saying goodbye isn't for everyone, it's certainly worth considering.

The New Funeral

As the *New York Times* reported on July 20, 2006, funerals have taken on a party atmosphere with marching bands, ice cream cones, and disco balls. Quoting Mark Duffey of Houston, the article noted that "Baby boomers are all about being in control...this generation wants to control everything from the food to the words to the order of the service. And this is one area where consumers feel out of control." The July 2006 issue of *Entrepreneur* reported on several funeral businesses, offering everything from space burials to burial on a coastal reef to carbonizing your ashes into a diamond. As funerals go, it seems the sky's the limit, literally.

Without guidance, families struggle. A colleague remarked, shortly after her mother's death following a decade-long battle with cancer,

> *You would think she might have mentioned what she wanted after all these years. So, instead of knowing, we agonized over what type of service, what she should wear, everything. It was horrible.*

The most critical decision is whether you wish to be buried or cremated. This decision often depends on your religious or cultural preferences. Once you've made this decision, the next step is to determine which funeral home will best serve your needs. Most funeral homes are full-service entities that can provide as few or as many services as you would like. They are trained professionals who will work with your family in determining any details you have not already decided upon. Many funeral homes offer prepaid funeral arrangements. Whether this is a good financial investment should be decided on a case-by-case basis and depends on your personal circumstances and your likelihood of remaining in the same geographic area.

Dan Rohling, CFSP, a licensed funeral director and embalmer, and author of *Funeral Information: A Consumer Guide*, says the most important thing to consider when selecting a funeral director is his or her responsiveness. Ask questions and inquire as to prices. All funeral directors are required to give you this information thanks to the Federal Trade Commission's 1984 Funeral Rule. As you learn the costs, keep in mind that the average cost of a funeral in the U.S. today is between $5,000 and $7,000, depending on where you live. If you aren't pleased with the answers, don't develop a rapport with the funeral director or feel "pressured," contact another funeral director. Mr. Rohling also suggests including an impartial third party in the discussions. He advises:

> *We all have an aversion to dealing with death. A neutral third party can help you focus on the task at hand and ask the tough questions, including questions regarding prices.*

Ask the funeral director to step out of the room so you can confer and make the best decisions, including cost considerations. Let the funeral director know if you're a veteran. Special benefits, including a flag, are available at no additional cost to honor those who served our country. The Funeral Consumers Alliance Web site at www.funerals. org also provides helpful information.

Talk with your spiritual advisor regarding the type of service or memorial that reflects your life and your beliefs. Discuss full religious Masses versus memorial services or celebrations of life. Your family priest, minister, rabbi, or cleric addresses these issues every day and is an excellent resource. He or she can help you decide the service's speakers, music, passages to be read, and tone. Ask your family members what's important to them, but the final decisions are yours.

The High-Tech Funeral

A funeral home in New York State now offers live funeral Web casts to far-away mourners. Who knew paying our respects would make it to the Internet!

Don't limit your planning to the religious or spiritual event. Consider the post-funeral gathering—the wake, sitting shiva, or visiting hours. John, age 68, left a Letter of Instruction that requested no religious service, but instead a "memorial party" not to exceed a maximum cost of $15,000. It's so important to John that his death be a celebration of his life that he's memorialized his intentions in a binding legal document. Lucas, age 52, went so far as to plan the menu and beer to be served. Robin, age 58, has her send-off planned as well:

I don't want a traditional viewing and funeral. I plan to be cremated, have a nice colorful urn, and then throw one hellacious rock and roll party to celebrate my life.

On the other hand, if you'd rather the event be private, say so.

Memorial Stone

A woman's husband dies. He had left $30,000 to be used for an elaborate funeral. After the event, the woman stated that she used the entire $30,000: $6,500 for the funeral, $500 for the church, $500 for the wake, and $22,500 for the memorial stone. A friend exclaimed, "How big can a memorial stone be for $22,500?" The widow's response: "Four and a half carats."

Practically speaking, during the service and post-funeral gathering, we advise that your family arrange for a trusted individual to mind your residence. Unfortunately, many unscrupulous individuals read funeral notices and decide that it's time to "pay a visit" (also known as a burglary). This is a considerable problem and not one to be ignored. It's important to protect your home and the home of your loved ones during all services.

Saying goodbye isn't easy. It's agonizing and painful. By leaving your letters and lessons of love, instructions, and intentions for your loved ones, you won't take away their grief, but you will make the process less burdensome.

Legacy Wants

- Prepare Letters and Lessons of Love.
- Write Letters of Instruction.
- Make funeral plans.

17

Legacy Wishes: Assisting Family, Friends, and Future Generations to Remember

How we create memories for our loved ones is as individual as our fingerprints. Some may be remembered by a funny story, others by a poem, and still others by a special song. Think of the beauty of the legacies left by musicians George Harrison and Warren Zevon in their respective last recordings. Both rock legends spent their final days writing and recording songs that shared their reflective experiences fighting cancer as well as ballads of love and hope for those left behind. Former Beatle George Harrison's emotional last album, *All Things Must Pass*, includes tributes to God, pronouncements of love, final goodbyes, and a lesson in "The Art of Dying."

All Things Must Pass

All things must pass

All things must pass away

All things must pass

None of life's strings can last

So, I must be on my way

And face another day

—George Harrison

Deborah Cumming wrote of her experiences with dying in a memoir titled *Recovering from Mortality—Essays from a Cancer Limbo Time.* In her beautiful writings, she shared her frustrations, her joys, her fears. She wrote,

> *I was undergoing a transformation…I can make choices…It is death that keeps me alive…I have something to do, to live the life I have. I'm busy with my task…*

We encourage you to follow these examples. Whether your death is imminent or not, share your love, lessons, and life experiences with your family and friends. You don't need the talent of a superstar to do this. You're a superstar in the eyes of your loved ones. Give them what they want: a piece of you.

We encourage you to share your personal history. You can do this through stories and sagas from your life experiences. Part of your personal history is your family tree. We'll help you get started so you can teach your loved ones not just about you, but also about where you came from. Lastly, in Chapter 18, "Your Legacy Wills: Your Safety, Your Rights, and Your Records," we'll explain why you may want to record this wonderful information for future generations, but why you also shouldn't record *everything*. These days, identity theft is rampant. Identities are being stolen from everyone, including the dead. We'll give you tips on how to protect yourself and your personal information.

A Guide to Your Personal Identity

When asked for your identity, what comes to mind first is probably your name and social security number, or maybe a fingerprint. Although technically this is part of your identity, it hardly begins to describe you. Your identity, instead, is more about your personal legacy. It's the lessons learned and taught, the love shared, and the life lived. It's your career; your personal milestones, no matter how big or small; your family and friends. It's your ideas. It's what makes you *you*.

Many of us have a tendency to shy away from discussions about who we are. We're self-conscious. We're not braggers. Or maybe we think that baking the blue ribbon pie at the local fair isn't worth mentioning. Besides, you may be thinking, who cares about that anyway? We disagree. And we're sure your loved ones do as well. You have much to teach and share. Every personal story contains a lesson and a moral from which others can benefit. If nothing else, it's an opportunity to pass along memories and share the joy of remembrance. So take the time to discuss your past—experiences and accomplishments—as well as your beliefs and values.

Getting Started

Don't know where to begin writing your personal legacy? Pick up *The Story of a Lifetime—A Keepsake of Personal Memoirs*. The book asks almost 500 questions about everything from relationships to jobs to milestones to help you get started. The leatherbound version is available at www.orvis.com or www.redenvelope. com. The soft cover (and less expensive version) is available at www.redenvelope.com or www.amazon.com.

If your loved ones are close by, invite them for story evenings. Share special recollections from your youth: the events you're proud of, the events you're not so proud of, your greatest achievements, your greatest regrets. If you don't know where to begin, ask yourself the following question, "What's the one lesson I've learned that I want to disclose so no one makes the same mistake I made?" Or think back on a funny event from your school days. If it makes you laugh, it will make your family laugh. Your loved ones want to know and remember as much as possible about you. It's time to fill them in on the life you've lived and the identity you've created.

Pass along tales of your elders—grandparents, great aunts, great uncles—and your friends. What was it like growing up during the Depression? Fighting in the Vietnam War? Being the only girl in a family of six brothers? We love hearing our parents reminisce about sitting in the bathtub in the dark while air raid sirens rang out during World War II. If face-to-face gatherings aren't possible, try videotaping your stories or at the very least writing them down. Ask a friend or family member to tape your stories and transcribe them if that's easier for you. Consider this your own personal identity protection.

The next thing most like living one's life over again seems to be a recollection of that life, and to make that recollection as durable as possible by putting it down in writing.

—Benjamin Franklin

In addition to your life experiences, your identity is made up of your ideas and values. Explain why you believe in a hard day's work, philanthropy, or volunteering. Why do you value saving every penny or, alternatively, sharing your good fortune with others? If you've benefited from traveling the seven seas, describe why you believe it's important. Each one of us has ideas that we've formed during our lifetime, no matter how long or how short. Each idea is as unique and as individual as we are. Your history, experiences, and ideas create your personal identity and legacy. We benefit from the legacies of others. Think back on what you learned from your friends and family. Be sure to share your life with your loved ones.

A Guide to Family Tree Preparation

Remember those old family stories told by your grandparents and your great aunts and uncles? You know, the tales of your great-grandmother being chased by a bear in Yosemite National Park in the 1920s or the ones told by your grandpa while you were out fishing on the Michigan lakes? Well, you may remember. But the only way your kids and grandkids will is if you tell them.

The best place to start is by creating a family tree. Begin by writing down everything you know about your elders—names, birthdates and places, and everything else you can find. We suggest using index cards for each person. Leave information blank if you don't know it. If you're not sure about something, write it down and title it aunt "A" or cousin "C" until you can come up with more.

Once you have your initial information, start your research by asking family members what they remember. Take advantage of any older relatives who may recall different stories or give you clues as to where to research missing information. Once you've tapped this resource, we suggest heading to the Internet.

The Internet has become a wonderful resource for genealogy, with both free and paid services to give you a hand. At http://rootsweb.com, you can access the Social Security Death Index, which allows you to determine the date and location of death for everyone who has died with a social security number. Having both the last known address of a deceased relative, as well as the state in which his or her social security number was issued, is extremely helpful. Old obituaries, which can be found at www.legacy.com/obituaries.asp, are wonderful sources of information. They usually list the place of residence of someone who has passed, as well as surviving relatives, giving you more branches on the family tree.

The Church of Jesus Christ of Latter-day Saints sponsors a free Web site (www.familysearch.org) that provides census, marriage, birth, and other records. For records that aren't yet digitized, you can visit the Family History Library in Salt Lake City, Utah. There are also over 4,000 family history centers in 88 countries. You can find out more at www.familysearch.org. A similar free service is available in Israel from My Heritage Ltd. (www.myheritage.com). Additional information on Jewish ancestors is available at www.jewishgen.org. Many of our ancestors came to this country from Europe, often by boat. The first point of entry for most was Ellis Island in New York. Log onto www.ellisisland.org for information about passenger arrivals, for example.

In addition to the many free Web sites, several genealogy sites offer subscriptions. The prices can be hefty, but they can be great resources for census records, immigration records, and information posted by other amateur genealogists. Try www.ancestry.com or http://geneaology.com. If you really get into it, the Elderhostel travel program (www.elderhostel.org) offers vacations focusing on genealogy, with trips to specific areas and classes on how to get started. Adult education programs often offer classes on genealogy. There are also many resources at your local library and bookstore. If you're not one for the books, professional genealogists are available, often at a steep price, to do the digging for you. But in our opinion, it's much more fun to do it on your own!

Today many companies offer DNA testing to help family historians find out more about their roots and ancestors. How does it work? Contact the company that you're interested in working with, and it will send you a kit to take your own DNA sample—usually a swab of the inside of your cheek—which is returned by mail. Most test for Y-chromosome markers. The number of markers tested varies from company to company (from 12 to 43). There is also an SNP (single nucleotide polymorphism) test that you can request. An SNP test looks for a genetic error that can help identify certain ancestral groups. Just beware! When you provide these firms with your DNA, it's no longer your protected health information. If you're still interested, some of the companies offering DNA testing are Family Tree

DNA (www.familytreedna.com), EthnoAncestry (www.ethnoancestry. com/index.html), and DNA Heritage (http://dnaheritage.com). You can also check out the National Geographic Society Genographic Project (www3.nationalgeographic.com/genographic/index.html).

Once you have your family tree in place, attach your favorite stories to each family member. Our parents put together wonderful family albums with a photo of each family member as well as some short remembrances. It's a piece of family history that we cherish.

Whether your goodbyes are imminent or a long time from now, sharing your personal legacy and your family history fulfills the wants, wishes, and wills of your loved ones. They want to know about you. They wish for your guidance and lessons. Use your will to make it happen.

Legacy Wishes

- Outline your personal identity.
- Research your family tree.

18

Your Legacy Wills: Your Safety, Your Rights, and Your Records

You might be wondering why, in a book about medical and legal planning, we're writing about your safety, privacy, and records. It's because, just like your leg bone being connected to your knee bone, your safety, privacy, and records are integral parts of your health care. And because doctors and lawyers have played a role in improving health care quality, it seemed a natural fit to fill you in on these important topics, along with your rights as a patient.

A Guide to Medical Safety

Whether we're boarding an airplane, jumping onto the country's most extreme rollercoaster, or buying ground beef, we want to know that we're safe—that the service or product we're purchasing is of the highest quality. The same holds true for our health care.

The patient safety and quality movement moved closer to center stage after the Institute of Medicine released its report, "To Err Is Human: Building a Safer Health System," in November 1999. Since then, quality reporting has been on the rise with the implementation of at least nine major programs focusing on quality parameters. The centerpiece of these programs has been counseling and screening. Other quality standards look at the physical plant (cleanliness and safety), satisfaction with physicians, and the performance and safety of nurses. Believe it or not, the number-one safety issue is determining a patient's name. Why? Getting the name right is critical. It means the right patient gets the correct drugs, treatments, and therapies. You might be asking how someone could get the name wrong. It's easy: Marie Smith or Maria Smith, Shawn Glisson or John Gleason, Wynne Whitman or Wayne Whitman. If you've been admitted to a hospital recently, you may have noticed that you're asked repeatedly for your name and even asked to spell it. Now you understand why hospitals are asking. Some institutions use bar codes on patient wristbands—be sure you're wearing the right one.

From 2002 to 2004, the Centers for Medicare and Medicaid Services (CMS) and the Department of Health and Human Services (HHS) conducted a volunteer incentive program, known as the Quality Initiative, in an attempt to measure quality in a new way. These measures were focused on the actual implementation of medical practices. There were five quality categories measured; three focused on the heart, one on orthopedic surgery, and one on infection. Hospitals in the top 50 percent were listed as top performers, with those in the top 20 percent receiving both recognition and a financial bonus. Hospitals performing in the bottom 20 percent received lower payments.

Since the results of the volunteer study were reported by the CMS, the U.S. Congress passed the Patient Safety and Quality Improvement Act of 2005, which was subsequently signed into law by President George W. Bush. The Act lays the foundation for better safety and quality reporting for hospitals and, in the future, doctors.

The final rules of the Act have not yet been determined, but the legislation is intended to help create a more open medical community willing to look at its inefficiencies. It will likely tie into the quality initiatives being instigated by CMS. With reimbursement to hospitals and doctors becoming more tied to quality standards, large databases of information will be accumulated.

This will create a new kind of public health department in the country. It won't be based only on reporting communicative diseases or bio-safety hazards. Instead, we'll have a system that pays providers for performance (also known as P4P). In the future, hospitals and physicians likely won't be paid as much unless they have documented proof that they've complied with quality and safety standards. There are additional incentives as well. Reporting institutions may receive additional Medicare funds for reporting compliance with quality standards. In addition, all compliance results will be reported both nationally and locally. You can already view the results for your hospital on the Internet at www.hospitalcompare.hhs.gov.

You can view the original study on which the hospital quality movement is based at the Web site for the Agency for Healthcare Research and Quality at www.ahrq.gov. If the volunteer study is any indication, the collected data would provide a resource for health care consumers to find out details about a particular hospital and the services it provides. For example, you could tell if a particular hospital were considered "qualified and safe" to treat infections by reviewing three parameters:

- Did the hospital report that its patients received pneumococcal vaccinations (a vaccine to prevent pneumonia that we're all supposed to get) every five years?
- Did the hospital report whether every eligible patient in the hospital had received a flu shot in the past year?
- Did emergency room patients with an infection receive an antibiotic within 4 to 8 hours of admission?

As with any study, there's always the possibility that the results reflect a reporting problem, not a compliance problem. Regardless, the future of health care and performance rewards is long overdue.

Our safety is critical to our well-being. We applaud these quality initiatives and look forward to great and measurable improvements in the near future.

A Guide to Patients' Rights

Our country is founded on a constitution that grants every man, woman, and child certain inherent rights. There are the amendments that we all memorized as kids, including the first 10 amendments known as the Bill of Rights. The ones we think of most are the right to free speech and the right to be free from unreasonable searches and seizures. Today, similar rights have been established for patients in the United States. These liberties offer us protections and opportunities. As with any purchase you make, it's important to understand what you're entitled to. Make sure you don't receive any less.

Patient's Bill of Rights

In 1999, the Patient's Bill of Rights was developed by the Department of Health and Human Services. Every patient is now encouraged to have the following protections:

- A right to be informed
- A right to choose providers and plans
- Access to emergency medical services
- A right to participate in treatment decisions
- Nondiscrimination and respect
- Health information confidentiality
- A right to complain and appeal decisions

Just creating a Bill of Rights, though, isn't enough. Significant improvements in health care communication are needed. To achieve these objectives, the medical, legal, economic, and technology communities must be encouraged to work together more.

The greatest challenge to achieving health rights for all Americans is the inability of different health information systems to communicate. Most of the blame can be placed on the lack of interoperability between different doctors and hospital records. A right to be informed, a right to participate in treatment decisions, and health information confidentiality are directly related to this challenge. To improve information systems, many initiatives have begun nationally to create an interoperable, private and secured, and personalized health record for every American. These large initiatives throughout the federal and state governments are trying to address the sometimes conflicting goals of such a system.

The conflicts currently being addressed are maintaining the privacy and security of your health records while allowing all who are supposed to see your records to do so in a timely fashion (interoperability). It also implies the ability to gain access to the part of your records your providers, for example, are allowed to see. In addition, these records need to be understandable (personalized) so that even the average patient can make informed decisions about his or her health care. Large amounts of planning and money will have to be spent to create an electronic health record that accurately represents your situations and needs, is private and secured, and is communicated to all your health providers, and no one else, in real time.

Although we should be supportive of such efforts, we must recognize that we have to be proactive with our own information in making it personal, protected, and private. Therefore, as we noted earlier in this book, we must make the time to create our own health care systems. We need to remain active and engaged in our health care by managing our own health care system with the assistance of our providers. The net effect is that we will become better health care consumers and hopefully enjoy better health in the process.

A Guide to Your Records

The reason that HHS is emphasizing interoperability of health care records is that unless you make sure that all your doctors, hospitals, and other health care providers are communicating, you should assume that much of the time they're not. Don't think that your physicians are going to know what's going on when you go to one hospital to get a biopsy, another to have a CT of your abdomen, and then another to see why your belly still hurts. Your physicians can't chase down these medical records, maybe because your records are dispersed, or perhaps because you can't remember the name of the hospital and the procedures and tests you had. Until medical, technological, legal, economic, and communication issues are resolved, you're still responsible for making your health care system interoperable.

So, what can you do? Keep a detailed record of your health care system and your protected health information as outlined in Chapter 1, "Health and Medical Wants: Your Personal Health Care System." Give this information to *all* of your providers and update this information on a regular basis.

The sometimes contradictory goals of interoperability, privacy and security, and personalization of health care records are at the heart of the health care delivery system's challenges today. These goals are far from being realized, and it is largely because of health privacy and security concerns. In 1974, the concept of privacy and security was applied to health information with the Privacy Act in an attempt to secure individuals' identities. With the explosive growth of medical treatments available to individuals came the realization that personalized health care, if not managed efficiently, would not be beneficial to patients or to those paying for such expensive treatments. Managed care plans were not successful in managing the care well enough to control expenditures.

The AIDS crisis created new privacy concerns. When a hemophiliac child in New Jersey was expelled from public school because of community fears, Congress acted to tighten the privacy of health information. With the safeguards on privacy and security of health information required by the Health Insurance Portability and Accountability Act of 1996 (HIPAA) and its Privacy Rule, an additional challenge faces those working toward making health records interoperable. Society has reasons to want its records to be seen by those who help us, but not by those who can hurt us. Do you really want your newly diagnosed heart arrhythmia known to the CEO when you are up for promotion in a competitive field? Your CEO may not understand the medicinal effects of Amiodarone in keeping your heart regular, and you could be passed over unfairly.

The concept of protected health information was consequently heightened in the health community's consciousness in recent years because of health discrimination. In the old days, there was a degree of privacy, generally because you had only one physician, records were rarely written down, and when they were, it was secure in one doctor's office. Doctor's bills were paid in cash or bartered for, so there were no insurance records. Literally, only the doctor knew all about you. In other words, you had privacy, but your personalized health care quality may have suffered.

Today we have medical progress that allows more diagnoses and more treatments, we have multiple physicians and providers, and we have electronic communications allowing information to be spread far and wide in the blink of an eye. Now that we have more information, we have more opportunities for mischief. Just ask Bill Clinton. In 2004, when our former president was a patient at New York-Presbyterian Hospital, at least 14 staff members inappropriately accessed his medical record. And with this mischief comes motive. Identity theft has become an extremely profitable crime. The use of an identifying number (a social security number) gives thieves the ability to bill for procedures never provided, simply by using a stolen social security number.

So why is confidentialty important? Unless you're an exhibition-ist, you value your privacy. You're not shouting at the top of your lungs, "I have herpes," "I'm HIV positive," or "I have six toes." We're not minimizing any of these conditions or trying to make light of them. We're simply demonstrating why your privacy is important. We're certain that there are some things you don't even want your doctor to know, so we're sure you don't want the world to know them either.

HIPAA imposes large fines on covered entities that disclose pro-tected health information. Although the possibility still exists that mistakes can be made and protected health information revealed, there has been a dramatic improvement in securing and protecting your privacy. HIPAA violations can be intentional (your health care provider selling a list of patients suffering from a particular condition to a marketing agency) or simply stupid (a staff person discussing a patient, by name, in a public elevator). Privacy is so important that, in the future, no new hospital will have a double room since, technically, a double room is a potential HIPAA violation.

Although your banker and brokers are most certainly electronic, most of your doctors probably aren't. Even if they're on the cutting edge of technology, there are major obstacles in obtaining and sharing your records with other members of your health care team. Having interoperable records is critical to improving health care. However, there are several barriers that we must overcome to make this happen.

The first barrier is privacy and security. Passwords, pass codes, and other traditional security measures are easily subverted. Thanks to HIPAA, privacy is paramount, so any old system just isn't good enough. The rest of the world is interoperable to a much larger degree; however, they're not required to meet and maintain HIPAA's privacy standards. We need a system that can verify the system user biometrically, can audit the information trail, and can verify the infor-mation entered into the system.

The second barrier is cost. Electronic health records are expensive, with the entities benefiting from interoperability rarely being the entities paying for the installation of electronic record keeping systems.

The third barrier is the lack of any common record keeping program among practitioners. Because the programs used today vary from office to office, integrating the systems is a technical challenge.

What Is a Covered Entity?

Under HIPAA, a covered entity is a health plan or a health care clearinghouse or provider who transmits any health information in electronic form.

Certain entities, like Web sites, are not covered by HIPAA—when you share your personal data, you've disclosed it with no requirement that your information be kept private. This means your info can be sold to marketing groups or other entities that want to buy it. Drug companies want this information. They benefit by understanding who buys what. The result has been, at least in our opinion, underhanded methods to learn more about you. One corporation funded a registry for individuals with head and neck cancer with a promise to help patients. Each doctor registering a patient received $1,000. Because the patient's consent wasn't required, providing this information could be a HIPAA violation.

A leading, private, national insurance company was touting a new search engine technology whereby a physician could send all of his or her office-generated electronic records, such as transcriptions of typed records, to another company to create a usable database. The doctor contracted with the third-party company, but all costs were paid by the insurance company with the understanding that the insurance company would only look at their insured individuals within the database for the purposes of predicting risks. This is another potential HIPAA violation, with the doctor being at risk if the third-party computer company holding the patient's data allowed it to be shared or sold. HIPAA regulations are complicated, involved, and extremely detailed. For the average physician who is already overworked, understanding the law isn't a top priority. This gives creative entities the ability to manipulate protected health information from unsuspecting physicians.

Medical Identity Theft

With health care costs skyrocketing, stealing an identity to get medical treatment is on the rise. Guard your insurance card like a credit card. If it's lost, report it immediately. Request an annual report of benefits paid to make sure no one's posing as you at a provider's office.

It may seem ridiculous to speak of "preserving health privacy" when 26.5 million patients in the Veterans Affairs Medical Center system had their identities lost or stolen in 2006 and other forms of identity theft are commonplace. (Fortunately, the VA thief only wanted the computer and didn't realize the value of the information he had.) The Office for Civil Rights within the Department of Health and Human Services has established instructions for filing a complaint for the loss of medical privacy. A complaint should be e-mailed to OCR-Complaint@hhs.gov if you believe that a person, agency, or organization covered under the HIPAA Privacy Rule violated your (or someone else's) health information privacy rights or committed another violation of the Privacy Rule. Remember, don't do it for the money. You won't get any. It is best to discuss this with your health care provider (your doctor or hospital, for example) rather than calling for a government investigation. Remember, the law and community standards may not yet be in sync. It's a difficult standard to always meet.

Just remember, though, that your privacy shouldn't extend to your providers. You should tell your providers everything. Not only are they required to keep the information private, but they also must make every effort to keep it secure.

A Guide to Personal Information Storage

These days we live in a high-tech, fast-paced society. Many of us rely on computers, wireless devices, and the Internet every day. Digital storage, digital records, digital everything—we're on our way to a paper-free society. The companion to this technological revolution is a new form of crime: identity theft. Identities can be stolen in a variety of ways, from the traditional stolen wallet to dumpster diving (recovering personal information from trash receptacles) to computer hacking. The ingenuity of today's modern criminal is impressive; if only they'd put these talents to good use instead of evil.

That's why we encourage you to protect yourself. Shred documents when you throw them out. Keep personal information in a secure location. When using your computer and secure Web sites, don't leave passwords and pass codes where they can be easily located. Change your passwords regularly. Use a combination of letters and numbers. And make the passwords distinctive. Using your birthday isn't exactly unique, is it? Neither is using the name of your child. Keep your firewall and other security measures on your computers up-to-date. Don't send your social security number in an e-mail—to anyone.

If you're going to use a Web site to store your personal information, including your protected health information, inquire as to the security and privacy of this information. Make sure information about you isn't being compiled or sold. Confirm security levels. Be sure that if you're using a wireless connection at your favorite coffee house or hotel that the connection is secure. We're not trying to frighten you; we're trying to make you aware.

The need for security extends beyond the end of your life. There are many recorded incidents of personal information (addresses, maiden names, and places of employment, for example) being taken from obituaries to be used on applications for car loans and credit cards. The social security death index, noted earlier, lists not only dates of death, but actual social security numbers. Since 9/11, most institutions providing death certificates, birth certificates, and licenses have implemented restrictions on who can obtain these documents. However, the clever still manage to find a way. Thieves have no problem going after the dearly departed. Talk to your loved ones about tightly managing your assets after your death to be sure that no new debts appear. Your credit cards should be cancelled immediately. Your financial institutions should be alerted. Vigilance is paramount.

Until we have systems in place to electronically identify forms and endorse each system user biometrically, we will never have complete security. We hope that in the future every computer will require the user to identify himself or herself, not through passwords and pass codes, but through the use of a fingerprint or other biometric identifier that is converted into another pass code. This will ensure the protection of our personal information and our protected health information. It will also provide a means to audit all computer access to ferret out the criminals.

With all of that said, we want you to be aware. We want you to be aware of the importance of safety and the war being waged to improve quality. We want you to know your rights as a patient. And we want you to understand that electronic medical records are on the way—with both benefits and detriments. The more you know, the better off you are.

Legacy Wills

- Research the quality and safety of your medical facilities.
- Understand your rights as a patient.
- Learn about the future of electronic health care records.
- Safeguard your personal information.

Conclusion

Throughout *Wants, Wishes, and Wills*, we've tried to provide you with two things: the tools needed to build your own health care system and to get your affairs in order, and the encouragement to talk, talk, talk about everything with your health care providers, family, friends, counselors, and everyone else who matters to you.

Growing up, we were taught that there were certain things you just "didn't talk about." Back then, the subjects were sex, religion, and politics. Turn your TV to any channel, and you'll see that these rules of polite conversation don't apply anymore. Few topics are taboo anymore, with the exception of death and our end-of-life wants, wishes, and wills.

So how do we venture into these emotional waters? Start by wading. Stick your big toe in with abbreviated conversations about the general subjects. Talk about a story in the news or the experience of a friend or neighbor. The next time, briefly weave your wishes into the conversation. As your loved ones develop a comfort level with the subject, spend more time explaining your desires. And keep talking about them. Even though it's written down, you'll avoid misunderstandings and miscommunications if you keep the conversation going.

Almost everyone who completed a survey we conducted had the same concern—"dying with dignity." Dignity is defined as "the quality or state of being worthy, honored, or esteemed." Tell your kids, parents, siblings, and friends that the best way to honor you is to listen. What if your loved ones still run screaming from the room, put their hands over their ears like we all did when we were five-years-old, or simply change the subject? Don't give up. As uncomfortable as it is, keep on bringing up the subject. Wait for a long car ride or other situation when you have your family members held captive. As they say, where there's a will, there's a way.

Classy Communicating

Even etiquette experts understand the importance of talking! Elizabeth L. Post in *Emily Post's Etiquette* writes,

Keeping open lines of communication among family members is the best way to avoid problems and to solve them when they do arise….Remember, however, that a good communications system requires a receiver as well as a sender.

The same need for conversation isn't limited to your family and friends. Express your desires to your health care providers. Harvard Medical School's *A Guide to Living Wills and Health Care Proxies* encourages individuals to verbally express their wishes to their physicians, even scheduling an appointment for the sole purpose of explaining your wants, wishes, and wills at the end of life. Let your counselor know exactly what it is that you want. Spell it out, not only in writing but with the spoken word.

We also hope that we've inspired you to take control of your life. As Deborah Cumming noted in *Recovering from Mortality—Reflections from a Cancer Limbo Time*:

> *From the outset, I felt that I had work to do. Certain tasks jumped to the top of the To Do list. And above the practical "set your affairs in order" tasks came the urgent, primordial command to "make your peace with God." I signed up for a cram course in death and life: I was the student, the teacher, and the subject matter. I had to make haste but slowly; whatever time there was—my lifetime—was what I needed....*

Even if death is decades away, taking control of all aspects of your health and legal affairs will give you the peace of mind to get out there and enjoy life without worrying about what you haven't done.

So how can you take control? By taking action. Understand your limitations. Focus on what you can do to improve your individual situation. Create your own health care system and interoperable health network and share it with *all* of your health care providers. Carry an up-to-date list of all of your medications with you to every appointment. Keep a record of your health care history, including recent tests, location of testing, and test results, if known.

With regard to your health and legal affairs, draw up a Living Will and Health Care Proxy. Share them with your health care providers and loved ones. Sign a Power of Attorney so that you can lean on friends or family members if you're unable to take care of your finances and other business matters yourself. Establish an estate plan to distribute your property on your passing. Make sure you have a valid and current will. Establish trusts for your kids, grandkids, friends, and other family members. Name a guardian to care for minor or disabled children. Leave a detailed Letter of Instruction. Reveal your personal history with your loved ones through Lessons and Letters of Love. Research your family tree. These are your wants, wishes, and wills. They're as unique as you are.

Your Wants, Wishes, and Wills

Your wants, wishes, and wills are important, not only to you, but also to those who care about you and care for you. They're composed of your information—medical, legal, and everything else. Your wants, wishes, and wills, whether recorded electronically or on good old-fashioned paper, should include the following:

- Your health care system
- Your medications
- Your health care history
- Your current health care situation—including recent tests, location of tests, test results, allergies and intolerances, and symptoms
- Your legal wishes—your Living Will, your Health Care Proxy, and your Power of Attorney
- Your last wishes—your will and trusts
- Your Lessons and Letters of Love
- Your Letters of Instruction
- Your other personal information—your personal legacy and family tree
- Your religious and philosophical beliefs
- Everything else that's important to you

Organizing this information, as we've said, is critical to improving both your medical and legal situations.

Because your wants, wishes, and wills are all about you, it's important to secure this information, whether you do it electronically or on paper. Back up electronic files. Keep paper copies in a fire box. Limit access to those who need to know.

You may be feeling overwhelmed by all of our suggestions in this book. We know that we've given you an incredible amount of information to digest and then address. And if we can't convince you to do all of this for yourself, we hope we've encouraged you to act for your loved ones.

Throughout this book, we've talked about taking charge—being the quarterback of your health care team and then picking your team; choosing individuals to act for you if you can't; naming guardians; deciding who gets your assets. It's been a continuous call to do, do, do something—anything. We've been nagging, aggravating, and probably downright annoying. Why? Because we believe in taking control. Every day we encounter people who don't plan, who don't take control, who do nothing. The result is additional frustration, upset, and trouble not only for our patients and clients but for their loved ones. That's why we want you to act, and act now. Life is a circle. It's up to each of us to complete our own circle of life. You can do this by implementing your wants, wishes, and wills.

That's why we wrote this book. Death and disease aren't fun. We don't want to deal with them, and it's clear that most of us don't want to talk about them. No question, it's much more enjoyable to talk about our upcoming vacation or our daughter's tremendous success in school. But we need to talk about death and disease—for ourselves and for our loved ones. We hope that *Wants, Wishes, and Wills* has inspired you to do just that.

Your Wants, Wishes, and Wills

- Talk, talk, and talk some more about your wants, wishes, and wills.
- Create (and update!) your wants, wishes, and wills.
- Take control of your health, your affairs, and you.

Additional Resources

In preparing for this book, we read countless materials by other authors. The following are our favorites. They provide comfort, resources, and different viewpoints on the end of life.

Suggested Readings List

Dying Well by Ira Byock, M.D. (New York, Riverhead Books, 1997).

Ending Life—Ethics and the Way We Die by Margaret Pabst Battin (New York, Oxford University Press, 2005).

Finding Your Way to Say Goodbye—Comfort for the Dying and Those Who Care for Them by Harold Ivan Smith (Notre Dame, Indiana, Ave Maria Press, Inc., 2002).

Funeral Information: The Consumer Guide by Dan Rohling, CFSP (Nampa, Idaho, Walter Andrew Publishing, 1990).

How We Die—Reflections on Life's Final Chapter by Sherwin B. Nuland (New York, Vintage Books, 1993).

Living Wills & Health Care Proxies by Martin M. Shenkman & Patti S. Klein (Teaneck, New Jersey, Law Made Easy Press, LLC, 2004).

On Death and Dying by Elisabeth Kübler-Ross, M.D. (New York, Scribner, 1969).

Parlay Your IRA into a Family Fortune by Ed Slott (New York, Penguin Books, 2005).

Recovering from Mortality—Essays from a Cancer Limbo Time by Deborah Cumming (Charlotte, North Carolina, Novello Festival Press, 2005).

Talking About Death Won't Kill You by Virginia Morris (New York, Workman Publishing Company, Inc., 2001).

The Needs of the Dying by David Kessler (New York, HarperCollins, 1997 [originally published under the title *The Rights of the Dying*]).

The Retirement Savings Time Bomb…and How to Diffuse It by Ed Slott (New York, Penguin Books, 2003).

The Ultimate Gift by Jim Stovall (Colorado Springs, Colorado, RiverOak, 2001).

What Dying People Want—Practical Wisdom for the End of Life by David Kuhl, M.D. (New York, PublicAffairs, a member of the Perseus Books Group, 2002).

Who Gets Grandma's Yellow Pie Plate Workbook by University of Minnesota Extension Service (Minneapolis, Regents of the University of Minnesota, 1999).

Web Site Resources

AARP—www.aarp.org

Agency for Healthcare Reporting and Quality—www.ahrq.gov

American Bar Association Lawyer Locator—www.abanet.org

American Board of Medical Specialties (ABMS)—http://abms.org

American Cancer Biorepository—www.theacb.com

American College of Trust and Estate Counsel—www.actec.org

Ancestry.com Genealogy Resource—www.ancestry.com

Blood Donor Information—www.givelife.org

Body Mass Calculator—www.nhlbisupport.com/bmi/

DNA Heritage—www.dnaheritage.com

Elderhostel Travel Programs—www.elderhostel.org

Ellis Island Genealogy Resource—www.ellisisland.org

EthnoAncestry—www.ethnoancestry.com/index.html

Family Tree DNA—www.familytreedna.com/

FDA Side Effect Reporting—www.fda.gov/medwatch/

Funeral Consumers Alliance—www.funerals.org

Funeral Planning Information—www.funeralinformation.net

Genealogy.com Genealogy Resource—http://geneaology.com

HealthGrades—www.healthgrades.com

Hospital Comparisons—www.hospitalcompare.hhs.gov

Institute for Safe Medication Practices—www.ismp.org

Internal Revenue Service—www.irs.gov

JewishGen: The Home of Jewish Genealogy—www.jewishgen.org

Joint Commission on Accreditation of Healthcare Organizations—
www.jointcommission.org/

Legacy.com Obituary Resource—www.legacy.com/obituaries.asp

Martindale-Hubbell Lawyer Locator—www.martindale.com

Medicare—www.medicare.gov/default.asp

My Heritage Genealogy Resource—www.myheritage.com

National Academy of Elder Law Attorneys—www.naela.com

National Cancer Institute—www.cancer.gov

National Geographic Society Genographic Project—
www3.nationalgeographic.com/genographic/index.html

National Institutes of Health Clinical Trials Service—www.
clinicaltrials.gov

National Marrow Donor Program—www.bonemarrow.org

Nutrition Information—www.nutrition.gov

Organ Donations—www.organdonor.gov

Personalized Health Care Status Web Sites—www.thestatus.com

RGK Center for Philanthropy and Community Service at the LBJ School of Public Affairs at the University of Texas at Austin—www. ServiceLeader.org/new

RootsWeb.com Genealogy Resource—www.rootsweb.com

Side Effect Resource—www.medlineplus.gov

Society of Financial Service Professionals—www.financialpro.org

The Church of Jesus Christ of Latter-Day Saints Genealogy Website—www.familysearch.org

USA Freedom Corps—www.usafreedomcorps.gov/

U.S. Preventive Services Task Force (USPSTF)—www.ahrq.gov/ clinic/uspstfix.htm

Veteran's Administration—www.va.gov

Volunteer Match—www.volunteermatch.org

Wants, Wishes, and Wills Web site—www.wantswisheswills.com

World Volunteer Web—www.worldvolunteerweb.org

Glossary

ACLS (advanced cardiac life support)—An advanced form of CPR using both mechanical and pharmaceutical interventions.

acute health condition—A disease or state of being for which there is a good chance of full recovery; usually an illness or condition of short duration.

administrator—The individual or financial institution appointed to oversee the estate of a person dying without a valid will or if no executor or personal representative is named. Also referred to as an *administratrix*.

Advance Directive—A document that combines both the Living Will directives and Health Care Proxy selection into a single document.

agent—Individual or individuals named to make your financial and business decisions under a Power of Attorney. Also called an *attorney-in-fact*.

allograph—Donation of tissue for someone else.

alternative—Refers to nontraditional methods of diagnosing, preventing, or treating disease.

antiarrhythmics—Interventions that stabilize heart rate and rhythm.

antibiotics—Drugs that were originally designed to fight infections. They may be administered by mouth (PO), vein (IV), or feeding tube.

anticoagulation agent—Drugs, such as Heparin or Coumadin, that thin the blood.

antihistamines—Interventions that reduce swelling by stopping allergic reactions.

antihypertensives—Interventions that lower blood pressure.

antihypotensives—Interventions that increase blood pressure.

arrhythmia—A heart having potentially dangerous abnormal beats.

artificial administered feeding and fluids—Nutrition and hydration provided to a person who cannot eat or drink on his or her own.

autograph—Donation of tissue for oneself.

beneficiary—The person who benefits from an estate, trust, insurance policy, or other asset.

beneficiary designation—A form that allows you to select a particular beneficiary to receive the proceeds from an insurance policy, retirement account, or other asset.

bequest—A small or specific gift made to an individual or charity in a will or trust, usually a dollar amount or specific item; also referred to as a *devise*.

board-certified physician subspecialist—A board-eligible subspecialist who has passed his or her respective specialty board.

board-certified specialist—A board-eligible specialist who has passed his or her respective specialty board.

board-eligible—A physician specialist who has completed his or her residency and is eligible to sit for the respective specialty board. If the physician specialist does not pass the specialty board within a set time frame after completing the residency, board eligibility will be lost, and the physician will be considered a non-board-eligible physician specialist.

board-eligible physician subspecialist—A physician subspecialist is a board-certified specialist in the specialty governing his or her subspecialty who has completed his or her fellowship and passed the necessary board examination within the required time frame.

brain stem—Part of the brain that governs basic bodily functions and reacts to the environment.

bronchodilators—Interventions that make the airway expand.

cardiopulmonary resuscitation (CPR)—A combination of rescue breathing and chest compressions delivered to patients when their heart is thought to stop beating (that is, cardiac arrest).

central line—A line placed in one of the large veins in the chest.

cerebellum—Back part of the brain that governs physical coordination of movement.

cerebrum—Part of the brain that controls personality, language skills, vision, memory, actual physical movements, and more.

chronic health condition—A disease or state of being for which there is likely no cure but that is not expected to cause death for at least six months or more.

circulation—The movement of fluid throughout the veins, arteries, and lymph system.

clinical research physician—A research physician most likely associated with a university, institutional review board, or pharmaceutical company, who performs clinical trials with new drug agents, devices, or protocols.

coma—Unconscious with no response to the external environment.

common disaster—Including a provision in a will or trust in the event that all your primary beneficiaries perish in a common disaster or prior to the decedent.

community property—Property owned by a husband and wife in a community property state.

complementary—Refers to nontraditional methods of diagnosing, preventing, or treating disease.

compression garments—Machine-operated pressure devices that help increase blood pressure and avoid clots.

conservatee—The incapacitated person whose affairs are managed by a conservator.

conservator—The individual appointed by a court to manage the affairs of an incapacitated person.

continuous positive airways pressure—Using a machine to force oxygen through a tube in your airway into areas of the lungs being underutilized.

convalescence—Recuperative processes of the body after an illness or injury.

corpus—The principal of a trust.

cortical brain—Higher brain function.

decedent—An individual who has died.

decongestants—Interventions that stop the production of mucus.

defibrillation—A process in which an electronic device gives an electric shock to the heart to reestablish normal contraction rhythms in a heart having dangerous abnormal beats (that is, arrhythmia) or in cardiac arrest.

delirium—Short duration episode of acute mental disturbance characterized by confused thinking and disrupted attention.

delirium tremens (DTs)—State of violent delirium induced by excessive and prolonged alcohol use.

dementia—Deteriorated cognitive function, often with emotional indifference.

devise—A small or specific gift made to an individual or charity in a will or trust, usually a dollar amount or specific item; also referred to as a *bequest*.

doctor—An individual with a medical degree, Ph.D., or other doctoral degree. Sometimes used to specify a physician with a medical degree only.

endotracheal intubation and ventilation—Putting a tube into the mouth or nose of a person who cannot breathe on his or her own and having a machine (or it may be done manually) breathe for the person.

cntcric intervention—An intervention method that helps patients receive hydration and nutrition.

escheat—Property that passes to the state on death as a result of dying intestate and having no living relatives at the time of death.

estate—All property and assets owned by an individual at death.

estate administration—The process of settling the estate of a deceased person.

estate planning—The process of ordering one's legal affairs to ensure the distribution of one's property and assets as one wants and wishes.

euthanasia—An active or passive act by an individual to end the life of another who is injured or horribly ill.

executor—The individual or financial institution that carries out the provisions of a will. Also referred to as an *executrix* or *personal representative*.

experimental physician—A basic research physician most likely associated with a university, pharmaceutical company, or government agency.

face mask—Mask that delivers pure oxygen into your nose and mouth.

fiduciary—An individual or financial institution acting for the benefit of an estate, trust, or person. Includes *executor, trustee, administrator*, and *guardian*.

fiduciary duty—The legal obligation of a fiduciary to act with trust and good faith.

gastric, duodenal, or jejunal tube—A feeding tube that goes into the stomach (gastric) or first (duodenal) or second (jejunal) part of the small intestine.

genome—The genetic code of a living being.

glucocorticoid steroids—Interventions that stop allergic reactions.

guardian—An individual granted the power to take care of the person and property of a minor or incapacitated person.

guardian ad litem—A special guardian appointed by a court to protect the interests of a minor or incapacitated individual during a court action.

Health Care Proxy—A legal document that appoints an individual, your health care representative, to make your medical decisions for you if you are unable. Also called a *Durable Power of Attorney for Health Care*, *Medical Power of Attorney*, and *Advance Directive for Health Care-Proxy Directive*.

health care representative—Individual named to make your health care and medical decisions under a Health Care Proxy.

health knowledge—Totality of information about health identity, health accounting, health registries, health research, health records, and health treatments as applied to any individual.

hemodialysis—Removing waste products from patients' blood when their kidneys aren't functioning.

high flow oxygen therapy—Using a face mask, nasal prongs, or cannulas to force oxygen into areas of the lungs being underutilized.

HIPAA—Health Insurance Portability and Accountability Act of 1996.

Holding Letter—A letter you write requesting your attorney to hold your original Power of Attorney documents until he or she is satisfied that you are incapacitated.

holographic will—A signed will written entirely in the handwriting of the person making the will that isn't witnessed or notarized.

hygiene—Prevention of disease and preservation of health.

informed consent—Requirement that you be told all aspects of a clinical trial or medical intervention, good and bad, and that your agreement to participate voluntarily be obtained in writing.

institutional physician—A business managing physician who runs an office practice, hospital staff, or other group of practicing physicians.

intangible personal property—Property which cannot be touched but has value; for example, stocks, bonds, securities, business interests, and money.

intestate—Dying without a valid will.

intubation—Interventions that place a tube in the mouth or nose to keep the airway open.

irrevocable—A legal document that can't be changed or revoked.

issue—All individuals born of a common ancestor. Your children, grandchildren, and great-grandchildren (and so on) are your *issue*. Also referred to as *descendants*.

joint tenants—Ownership of an undivided interest in a whole asset that automatically passes on the death of a joint tenant to the other surviving joint tenants.

licensed physician—A medical doctor who has completed one internship year, passed a state medical licensure board, and doesn't have criminal convictions in any state. A licensed physician without further training in residency, or before he or she completes residency training, may be referred to as a general practitioner.

licensed practical nurse (LPN)—A nurse who has completed a one- to two-year training program.

Living Will—A legal document that outlines your wishes regarding your medical care at the end of life. Also called an *Advance Directive for Health Care—Instruction Directive, Medical Directive*, or *Directive for Physicians*.

medical doctor—A medical school graduate who may or may not be qualified by a state, hospital, or with a given specialty or subspecialty. Also called a *physician*.

medicine—Medical diagnoses and subsequent treatment of disease.

metastasized—The spread of disease from the origination point of the disease to another part of the body.

minimally conscious—Altered consciousness with erratic, inconsistent responsiveness.

narcotics—Very strong painkillers, such as morphine.

nasal cannula—The small tube that is inserted in your nostrils. This delivers the smallest amount of oxygen.

nasogastric tube—A feeding tube inserted through the nose and passed into the stomach.

neurohormonal function—Loss of whole brain function.

nonnarcotic pain medication—Nonsteroidal, anti-inflammatory drugs (NSAIDs), including ibuprofen, aspirin, and acetaminophen.

numerical physician—A business-managing physician for health payers who is most likely associated with an insurance company, medical product development company, or government agency.

nurse practitioner—A registered nurse with advanced training in a particular medical specialty.

nutrition—Process by which the body assimilates and uses food for energy and growth.

otolaryngoscopy—Intervention that evaluates the nose and throat to find out what's blocking the airway.

outcome—The end result of treatment, which can be either positive or negative.

oxygen tent—A structure that encloses a patient in bed and provides an oxygen-rich environment.

pacemaker—A device that keeps the heart beating regularly.

palliative care—The treatment of pain.

paracentesis—Draining the abdomen to relieve pressure.

payable on death (POD) account—A designation on a bank or brokerage account or other asset that provides that the asset passes to the named POD individual on the owner's death.

PEG (percutaneous endoscopic gastrostomy)—A feeding tube placed using a scope passed into the stomach and a hole cut through the stomach wall and external abdominal skin.

per capita—Division of an estate among a single branch of the family tree, share and share alike. If you leave your estate to your children *per capita* and one of your children has already died, that child's share will be split among your living children.

pericardial window—Creating a site to allow the heart sack draining to take place.

pericardiocentesis—The draining of fluid from the heart sack to allow the heart to beat.

per stirpes—Division of an estate among all branches of a family tree. If you leave your estate to your children *per stirpes* and one of your children has already died, that child's share will pass to his or her children. Also referred to as *by representation*.

persistent vegetative state—Unconscious with eyes open and little response to the external environment.

personal representative—The individual appointed by a court to administer an estate; also called an *executor* or *administrator*.

physician—A medical doctor who has graduated from medical school or osteopathic school.

physician's assistant—A medical practitioner who works under the direct supervision of a doctor.

physician-assisted suicide—Situation in which a doctor enables a terminally ill patient to take his or her own life.

physician in fellowship—A board-eligible specialist who chooses to apply and is accepted for a particular subset of study within a given specialty. Fellowships can last from one to four years. For example, internal medicine fellowships include, but are not limited to, cardiology, pulmonology, medical oncology, endocrinology, rheumatology, gastroenterology, hematology, and infectious disease.

physician in internship—A medical doctor in the first year of a one-year accredited residency training program such as internal medicine, general surgery, or family practice.

physician specialist—A physician who has completed his or her residency program in a given area such as internal medicine, general surgery, pediatrics, family practice, and obstetrics and gynecology, for example.

physician subspecialist—A physician who has completed his or her fellowship program.

PICC line—A peripherally inserted center catheter placed into a large arm vein.

port—An implanted device that prevents multiple needle sticks in more painful areas of the body.

power of appointment—Power granted to a trust beneficiary to appoint the remaining trust assets to another on the death of the trust beneficiary.

practicing physician—A diagnosing or treating physician who sees patients regularly in an outpatient or inpatient setting.

principal—Individual signing a Power of Attorney, Health Care Proxy, or Living Will.

probate—Establishing the validity and authenticity of a Last Will and Testament before a judicial authority.

pro rata—Dividing based on percentage interest rather than equally.

psychosis—Basic derangement of the mind, including hallucinations, delusions, disorganized speech and behavior, and defective or lost contact with reality.

randomization—A process by which subjects in a clinical trial are assigned in no particular order to receive one of the treatments being studied.

real property—Land and everything located on the land.

registered nurse (RN)—A nurse who has completed a two- to four-year degree in nursing.

regulatory physician—An academically oriented physician involved with organizing basic research results, reimbursement policies, or clinical research to set best-practice guidelines for institutional and practicing physicians and providing organized feedback to experimental, numerical, and clinical research physicians.

relaxants—Pain medication to help patients feel more relaxed.

remainder—Value of a trust at the end of its term or at the death of a life or income beneficiary.

resident physician—A licensed physician or a foreign medical graduate (FMG) of a non-U.S. medical school who is in a residency program for a particular medical specialty. FMGs may receive their state medical license to become a licensed physician after completing a three-year residency, which includes a one-year internship, and passing a state medical licensure board, provided he or she doesn't have criminal convictions in any state.

respiratory support—The administration of extra oxygen through various mechanisms such as high-flow oxygen therapy (oxygen given by face mask or nasal prongs or cannulas), continuous positive airways pressure (forcing oxygen into areas of the lungs being underutilized), endotracheal intubation and ventilation (putting a tube into the mouth or nose of a person who cannot breathe on his or her own and having a machine breathe for the person), or a tracheotomy (a surgical incision in the windpipe).

revocable—A legal document that can be changed, amended, or cancelled.

Section 529 Plan—A tax-deferred education savings plan.

sedatives—Pain medication to help a patient sleep.

side effect—An unintended consequence of a drug, treatment, or procedure.

stage—Term used to discuss the severity of the progression of a disease.

subacute health condition—A health condition exists, but not all of the symptoms are evident.

suicide—The taking of one's own life intentionally and voluntarily.

surety bond—A bond insuring the performance of an executor, administrator, trustee, or other fiduciary.

surgery—Any invasive procedure or operation, especially one involving the removal or replacement of a diseased organ or tissue. Surgery may be minimal (such as the placement of a central line for IV access), major (such as open heart surgery), or somewhere in between.

tangible personal property—Property which you can touch and feel; for example, a car, jewelry, photographs, and sterling silver.

TEN (total enteral nutrition)—Feeding and fluids delivered directly to the gastrointestinal tract.

tenants by the entirety—Joint ownership of property with a right of survivorship that is only between a husband and wife.

tenants-in-common—Property ownership with other individuals that may or may not be equal, with the share of a co-tenant passing on his or her death pursuant to his or her will or by the laws of intestacy.

terminal health condition—A disease or state of being that is expected to end one's life within six months; also referred to as *end-stage*.

testate—Dying with a valid will.

testator—Individual who leaves a valid will at the time of his or her death.

TPN (total parenteral nutrition)—Feeding and fluids delivered by IV.

tracheotomy—An intervention that cuts a hole in the front of the neck to insert a tube directly into the airway.

trust—A legal entity that holds property for another person's benefit (the beneficiary). An *inter vivos* trust is established during life. A *testamentary* trust is established at death.

trustee—The individual or financial institution that administers a trust.

Uniform Transfers to Minors Act (UTMA) or Uniform Gifts to Minors Act (UGMA) Accounts—Accounts opened in the name of a minor that become available to the minor at the age of majority.

ventilator—The mechanical device that assists a patient to breathe by mechanically forcing oxygen into the lungs; also called *artificial respiration*.

ward—A minor or incapacitated person under the care of a guardian.

will—A legal instrument in which a person disposes of property at death.

Index

I

N

name of patient,
    determining, 242
narcotics, 88, 272
nasal cannula, 86, 272
nasogastric tube, 120, 272
National Academy of Elder Law
    Attorneys Web site, 175
national bone marrow
    registry, 142
National Cancer Institute Web
    site, 89
National Center for
    Complementary and
    Alternative Medicine, 75
National Geographic Society
    Genographic Project Web
    site, 239
national retail pharmacy
    chains, 26
natural remedies, lack of
    regulation, 53
neural tube defects
    counseling, 55
neurohormonal function
    defined, 272
    loss of, 105-107
neurologic history, 48
newborn vision counseling, 54
nonnarcotic pain medication,
    88, 272
nonpregnant females, counseling
    standards, 56
nonprogressive dementia, 98
nonrelatives, providing for,
    185-186
nontolerance, defined, 47
nonvoluntary euthanasia, 108
numerical physicians, 18-19, 272
nurse practitioners
    defined, 13, 272
    in national retail pharmacy
        chains, 27

nursing homes, 25
nutrition
    artificially administered
        feeding and fluids, 120
    counseling standards, 54
    defined, 90, 272
    enteric interventions, 90-92
nutritional intervention, 91

O

obesity counseling, 54
obesity screening, 59
obituaries
    family tree preparation, 237
    identity theft usage of, 252
obituary information in Letters
    of Instruction, 223
obstetric and gynecologic
    history, 49
obstetrics and gynecology
    counseling standards, 55
    screening standards, 60
Office for Civil Rights, 250
oncology
    counseling standards, 54
    screening standards, 58
oncology history, 48
ophalmologic history, 49
ophthalmology counseling
    standards, 54
organ donation, 140
    informed consent, 154
    Living Wills and, 124
    record keeping and
        reporting, 155
organization in estate
    administration,
        importance of, 164
original legal documents,
    storing, 128
orthopedic and rheumatologic
    history, 49

standard treatments
  clinical trials versus, 72-73
  receiving, 71-72
standards
  counseling standards, 54-57
  screening standards, 57-61
state estate taxes, 170
statistics, wills completed, 210
stem cells, adult, 141
storing original legal
        documents, 128
*The Story of a Lifetime—A
        Keepsake of Personal
        Memoirs*, 235
Stovall, Jim, 220
strabismus screening, 58
studies
  clinical trials versus, 65
  information donation for, 143
  informed consent, 153-155
  record keeping and reporting,
        155-156
subacute health conditions,
        34, 275
subspecialists, 22, 274
succession planning for small
        businesses, 213
suicide
  defined, 108, 276
  Living Wills versus, 122
  loss of will to live and, 103
supplemental benefits trusts, 184
surety bonds, 165, 208, 276
surgery, 121, 276
surgical interventions for pain
        relief, 88
symptoms, discussing with health
        care providers, 35, 47

T

*Talking About Death Won't Kill
        You* (Morris), 130
tangible personal property,
        196, 276
taxes
  charitable donations and,
        146, 188
  estate planning and, 170-174
  estates left to parents, 182
  federal estate taxes, 171-173
  federal generation skipping
        transfer tax, 171
  gift taxes, 213-214
  income taxes, 173-174
  inheritance taxes, 170
  IRAs as charitable
        donations, 190
  Section 529 plans, 183
  state estate taxes, 170
  trusts and, 203
  UGMA/UTMA accounts, 184
  in wills, 195
TEN (total enteral nutrition), 91,
        120, 276
tenancy by the entirety, 163, 276
tenancy-in-common assets,
        163, 276
terminal health conditions,
        34-36, 276
terminally ill patients, selecting
        hospice, 28-30
testamentary trusts, 205,
        211, 276
testate, 276
testators, 16, 276
testatrix, 16, 276

TURNING SILVER INTO GOLD
How to Profit in the New Boomer Marketplace
Mary Furlong

As they age, America's 78 million baby boomers will live more active, creative, inventive lives than any generation before them. This represents enormous business opportunities. In this book, one of the world's leading authorities on marketing to "post-50" baby boomers offers a complete blueprint for profiting from that opportunity. Dr. Mary Furlong reveals breakthrough product and service opportunities and gives you the tools, resources, techniques, and data you need to build a profitable business around them. Furlong draws on her experience leading SeniorNet and ThirdAge Media, as well as the Boomer Business Summit and $10,000 Business Plan Competition, where she has reviewed hundreds of new business plans targeting these emerging markets. *Turning Silver into Gold* offers powerful insight into baby boomers' new lifestyle transitions in housing, health, fitness, finances, family, fashion, romance, travel, and work, and the new brand choices they're about to make. Furlong shows how to segment baby boomer markets and find opportunities to innovate entirely new categories of products and services. You'll discover which sales and marketing strategies really work and even uncover opportunities in the surprising worldwide boomer market. Throughout, Furlong combines extensive, authoritative market research with inspirational case studies from passionate, tenacious entrepreneurs and brand leaders who are blazing new trails in these fast-growing markets.

ISBN 0131856987 ■ © 2007 ■ 304 pp. ■ $24.99 USA ■ $29.99 CAN

SAVING FOR RETIREMENT WITHOUT LIVING LIKE A PAUPER OR WINNING THE LOTTERY
Gail MarksJarvis

The perfect book for anyone who's concerned about saving for retirement, from baby boomers to "Generation Y." Most books on retirement investing are either too complex, too superficial, or too gimmicky to help you. Instead of starting with some lofty financial planning theory, the author walks individuals through the beginning of the process with IRAs and 401(k)s, leaving no basic questions unanswered. Instead of telling readers to open an IRA, as many books do, she tells them how to open one: where to go, what the forms mean, how to decide how to invest, the essential first steps. Then it moves to sophisticated investing strategies that are made simple with models. The goal is to remove everything from the readers' path that typically trips up regular people. Drawing on her email and telephone conversations with over 20,000 readers, she walks you step-by-step through the entire process. She teaches the key principles a professional financial planner would use, but makes them simple enough to apply on your own! From opening an account to choosing the right mutual funds, this book shows you exactly how to do it. One step at a time, you'll learn how to handle IRAs, 401(k)s, and other retirement savings wisely, set targets, make good decisions, and avoid costly mistakes. Even if you've never invested before, this book will build your confidence, so you can finally do what you've meant to do for years...get on the path to a secure and comfortable retirement!

ISBN 0132271907 ■ © 2007 ■ 272 pp. ■ $17.99 USA ■ $21.99 CAN